LEARNING

MEM

MICROSOFT ENDPOINT MANAGER

Unified Endpoint Management with Intune and the
Enterprise Mobility + Security Suite

SCOTT DUFFEY

CONTENTS

ABOUT THE AUTHOR

I am a Program Manager at Microsoft and I work on Microsoft Endpoint Manager features. My passion for the product started in the early days when it had a lot of wrinkles and was branded "Windows Intune". I am especially proud to witness its transition to awesomeness and ascension to the top-right of the Gartner Magic Quadrant (in case you don't follow industry analyst reports, this just means it's one of the best UEM products in market). In my first years at Microsoft, I worked in a customer-support type role as a Premier Field Engineer (PFE). I worked with a new customer each week – helping IT folks tweak their Windows desktop configurations through Group Policy or Configuration Manager to improve performance, security or end-user experiences. I jumped on the "Intune" train early because it seemed new and interesting, and I thought I could make this my new special skill. My managers at the time were all about something called a "T-shape", referring to a popular metaphor at the time for one's breadth and depth knowledge. The top of the T-shape represents your breadth skills and the lower portion represents depth. The idea was that you should have broad technical knowledge in some areas and deep knowledge in others. I was inspired to go deep on Intune, so I learned as much as I could and started teaching the customers I worked with, doing workshops and setting up proofs-of-concepts with them. At this stage, there was very little enterprise use or interest in Intune, and it was really all about mobile phones (including Windows Phone), not PC's. When Windows 8.1 came out there was a new cloud management stack on it and a lot of buzz around "Modern Management" where admins were encouraged to throw out all the management tools they knew and loved (Group Policy and Configuration Manager), forget all the skills they had learned and earned their living on over the last ten years and move to this new, shiny, simple thing in the cloud. That message did not go down well at all.

After about a year or so of Intune deployment with customers, I had an opportunity to move from "the field" into the Intune product group, in a new team called the Customer Acceleration Team (CAT). The idea behind this team was that Microsoft product groups could be directly engaged with large enterprise customers who were actively deploying Intune so that the engineering teams would gain a deep understanding of customer blockers and issues. Knowing about them sooner could fast-track important product development and prioritization. It was my job to work directly with a few special and large customers in the Asia region, understand their concerns and summarize the impact to the rest of the product team. I also helped those clients rapidly get Intune from proof-of-concept to fully deployed in their environments. There were perks to this job: the travel was fun and interesting, and I was no longer tied to an office. I worked from home 80 percent of the time and spent the rest travelling. Since I was covering the Asia region, I spent time onsite with customers from India to Japan and many across Australia. I also traveled to Microsoft headquarters in Seattle a couple of times a year to meet with the rest of my team, fill up the knowledge-tank on upcoming features and innovations and tap feature PMs on the shoulder for updates on blockers that were affecting my customers. I really enjoyed the CAT team but realized that I wanted to have a bigger role in the direction of the product and its features. On one of my trips to head office, I put out feelers and told a few folks that being a feature PM in Intune would be my dream job. Next thing I knew, I was boarding my family on a plane from Australia to start a new adventure at Microsoft head office in Redmond, Washington.

I have always had a passion for writing. I have blogged, written, and rewritten product documentation and too many product specifications to count – but never a book. When the COVID-19 pandemic broke out in March 2020, Microsoft was one of the first companies to close offices and send people home to work. I needed a creative outlet and writing this book helped me scratch that itch. It motivated me to get out of bed at 5am each morning in the dark cold in front of my computer, headphones on, cup of coffee in hand and a smile on my face. I was also motivated by the fact that there were no other Microsoft Endpoint Manager books yet. I knew admins around the world were struggling with the learning curve and I could help.

This book contains knowledge I have picked up over the years that I would gladly share with any MEM customers I meet or even new members of the MEM product development team who need to ramp up quickly. Thank you for reading it!

ACKNOWLEDGMENTS

So many people were involved in bringing this book to you – I am thankful to the people that contributed directly but also to the people in my personal and work life that gave me a leg-up at some point so that I could eventually write this book:

- Roger Southgate – my good friend and mentor. Thank you for your contribution as Chief Technical Reviewer for this book.

- Leaders and mentors – Callan Tenabel, my first hiring manager at Microsoft who took a chance when he hired me based on potential rather than experience. Ben Francis, Martin Morrison, Ian Bartlett, Bryan Keller and Heidi Cheng too – all Microsoft managers who pointed me in the right direction.

- My brother, Chad, for being a great role model in tech and one of the most generous people I know. I won't forget the things you do for me.

- My Microsoft colleagues and teammates, both developers and PMs, for patiently teaching me things I now can teach to others.

Lastly my wife, Mandy, for giving me the time and space to work on projects like this. Thank you.

CHAPTER 1

INTRODUCTION

Did you just land an IT job only to learn your new employer is using Microsoft Endpoint Manager (MEM) for device management? Perhaps you stretched the truth on your resume and suggested you knew it already? Maybe you are an old-hat, know-your-stuff device management pro for another product but your boss just told you the company is migrating? Whatever the case, this book will be your zero-to-hero ramp-up guide.

In authoring this book, I promise you a few things – firstly, I promise an easy but content-rich read. MEM is complicated enough without acronyms and tech-speak. I will keep it simple and articulate, and I'll take the time to explain industry terminology. Second, I learn by doing stuff (and breaking stuff) and so do most of the IT admins I know. To maximize learning, I will get you 'doing stuff' as much as possible. Exercises will not have fine-grained, explicit steps; instead, I will guide you through the flow and prevent you from getting stuck or breaking too much stuff. The book is structured to start out simple, adding building blocks as you go until you reach a point where you can fish for yourself. I recommend that you go beyond the basic steps provided and take regular detours to explore additional configurations, settings and features along the way. At the end of this book, you should be comfortable building-out full scenarios in lab or production environments and be ready to show your boss how awesome you are.

There is one promise I cannot make. MEM is a cloud service; it gets updated super-frequently (once a month, sometimes more). So frequently that some content will get stale. Features and entire products get renamed, new features get added or just annoyingly moved around the UX! You will be fine, though – I will teach you the broad stuff, the concepts and administration patterns and give you all the resources you need to stay up to date to handle the inevitable product changes so you can be your company's go-to MEM ninja for years to come.

Intune vs Endpoint Manager? What do we call this thing?

The first thing you need to know if you are new to this space is that the product name "Microsoft Endpoint Manager" is relatively new, and the product boundary is a little confusing – it's got history. The nuts and bolts of the MEM product have existed for a long time as two separate, but successful, products – Intune and Configuration Manager.

The cloud product – Microsoft Intune – was first launched as "Windows Intune" and, as the name suggests, initially only supported Windows device management starting with Windows 7. After expanding into other mobile platforms, it was re-branded to "Microsoft Intune".

Configuration Manager is probably the best-known enterprise device management software out there. It has gone by many names through the years, too, such as System Management Server (SMS) and System Center Configuration Manager (SCCM). Nowadays most IT pros just call it ConfigMan.

In 2019 there was a big announcement at the Microsoft Ignite conference – the two popular products announced to the IT pro world that they were getting married and birthing a beautiful new baby called Microsoft Endpoint Manager (MEM).

This product name stuff will be important background knowledge as you work your way through this book and any of the online docs and blog posts. You will find various names used out there and you might need to try alternative search terms to get the results you are looking for. In this book, I will be referring to the combined product as "Microsoft Endpoint Manager" (or MEM, for short), but I'll use "Intune" from time to time when talking about parts of the product that only exist in the cloud service and are not at all relevant to the on-prem Configuration Manager server scenarios and infrastructure.

Reading and doing

To get the most out of this book I recommend both "reading it" and "doing it". Take detours to try out new features you see along the way. You will find exercise sections called "Do it" as you progress, with steps getting less structured as you become familiar with the consistent patterns in the MEM admin center. In the first chapter, you will start by setting up a MEM trial account so you can really start sinking your teeth into it. Before you get there, though, there are some things that you will need.

Things you will need

Here is your equipment checklist:

- ✓ Administrator workstation
- ✓ Test devices (one of each platform you want to learn about)
- ✓ Internet connectivity and network
- ✓ (Optional) an on-prem network lab

Administrator workstation

This could be anything – PC, Mac – I do not mind, as long as it has good internet connectivity. On the admin workstation, you will need your favorite web browser installed to reach the administration portal. I recommend the Chromium-based Microsoft Edge browser for a few reasons: firstly, I have documented the lab steps with it; second, it has some neat features like the ability to add and switch profiles, which is super handy when logging into different cloud services with different personas.

Test devices

Here are my recommendations for test devices – you don't need to rush out and buy a whole stack of new devices (although this book might be a good excuse for you to do so!). When I first started learning MEM, I either asked my family if I could use their old ones or built virtual machines for Windows. If your boss is awesome, they will agree to let you buy this stuff for the good of the company.

- An iOS test device – if you or someone in your family has an old iPhone or iPad lying around you should be able to get by using that. If you need to buy a new one, know that you will be able to do all the exercises in this book using the cheapest you can get away with (I bought a new iPad Mini because my kids get annoyed when I remotely wipe theirs).

- A macOS test device – most folks I know buy one of these second-hand. If you do that just make sure it can run macOS X 10.13 or later, as that's the minimum supported by MEM at the time of writing. There are a couple other options if you do not want to buy a Mac, including renting one (online) through a service (around $50 per month for a dedicated device) or hosting a virtual machine in the cloud (AWS currently offers this instance type, but it's intended for developer use and just a bit on the expensive side right now).

- At least one Android test device – Microsoft recommends devices running Android 5.0 (Lollipop) or later but my recommendation for a smoother experience is to use no older than Android version 6.0 (Marshmallow). If you can swing it, I recommend getting your hands on more than one Android device so you don't have to constantly re-configure and re-enroll the device into different modes.

- A Windows device or VM – you will be able to get away with most exercises in this book with a VM (either VM in the cloud or a hypervisor like Hyper-V). In fact, I strongly recommend using a VM because it's faster to reset the environment after each exercise. There are just one or two exercises where a physical PC would be helpful; I'll note that in the "Do it" steps.

Note on minimum OS requirements

The minimum requirements for platforms are a moving target as most platforms bring out two major OS revisions a year. An up to date list of supported operating systems and browsers for Endpoint Manager is documented here: https://bit.ly/30SLIrL.

Networking

For most exercises in this book, you don't need to configure anything special for networking. A good internet connection (for your administration workstation and each of your test devices) is a great start. You won't need any of your test devices to have SIM cards – simply connecting to your home or work Wi-Fi is good enough. My recommendation is to connect using a Wi-Fi access point that is connected directly to the internet and not subject to a proxy or network-based firewall because submitting change requests to add new exceptions to your company's proxy is just going to slow down your learning.

"On-prem" environment

In Chapter 12 we will cover hybrid on-prem and cloud scenarios such as configuring Hybrid Azure AD Join and MEM Co-management for Windows 10 devices. This will involve connecting existing on-prem Active Directory and Configuration Manager environments to MEM. To complete those exercises, you should have access to a lab environment that imitates a basic on-prem Windows environment (with a domain controller, Configuration Manager server, and a Windows 10 client). The steps for setting up this lab environment on Azure VM's are covered in the step-by-step instructions but you may choose to bring your own instead. If you go down the route of spinning up an Azure virtual machine lab environment, you will need access to an Azure subscription and enough credit to run the VM's.

CHAPTER 2

GETTING STARTED WITH MICROSOFT ENDPOINT MANAGER

In this chapter, you will learn the MEM fundamentals. You'll get a quick run-through of the product scope and terminology and cover the day zero steps needed to get yourself set up with a MEM environment to learn with.

What is Microsoft Endpoint Manager (MEM)?

Microsoft Endpoint Manager (MEM) is a Unified Endpoint Management (UEM) product. Put simply, MEM is just a way for you, the IT admin, to manage all the different types of devices used in your organization. This includes PC's, virtual machines, mobile phones, tablets, kiosks, digital signage boards, and other types too.

When I say "manage", I am talking about things you do to them remotely from the comfort of your own web browser; some of these management tasks cause a change in the device's configuration – for example, deploying applications to them or making them apply specific security settings. Some device management tasks are read-only, such as producing a report detailing the boot and startup time for your Windows 10 devices and being offered insights and suggestions on how to improve. As you will read in this book, there are a plethora of things that you, the admin, might need to "manage" on your devices and MEM is your tool to do it all.

MEM is a cloud service – this means it's all on the web and companies like yours pay a subscription fee to use it. One of the great things about this is the lack of infrastructure needed to get started. Microsoft operates the cloud service so that you do not need to install anything on your on-prem servers. Microsoft takes care of all the hard stuff – high-availability, maintenance, and fault tolerance. They roll out the updates (including new features and capabilities) to the service incredibly regularly (once a month, sometimes more) and you have to do absolutely zero upgrade work to use them.

Subscriptions and licensing

The first step to using MEM is to acquire the right licenses to use it. This is achieved through a subscription. This subscription is specific to MEM – it's not part of any Azure subscription you may already use to create and manage Azure VM's or websites, for example.

There are three main subscriptions you can buy from Microsoft to get your hands on MEM and most of them have free 30-day trials:

Intune (Microsoft Endpoint Manager)-only license

This licensing option is rarely purchased, and I don't recommend it. It lacks some key integrations with other related services (for example, it does not give you the power to create the dynamic device groups you will almost certainly need in your Intune deployment, since that feature is part of the Azure AD Premium license).

Enterprise Mobility + Security (EMS) Suite license

This is a popular way for companies to get MEM. It includes a load of other products (the most important one is Azure Active Directory Premium). You will be able to work through almost all scenarios in this book using this subscription.

Microsoft 365 (E3 or E5)

The Microsoft 365 licensing suite has everything in the EMS suite, plus subscriptions for Microsoft Office 365. I recommend using the Microsoft 365 E5 subscription for lab setup because you will be able to work through everything in MEM, including end-to-end scenarios that require Office (for example, using Endpoint Manager, Azure AD Conditional Access, and Office to restrict access to sensitive documents stored on SharePoint Online).

Note that the above licensing information is super-focused and simplified to get you up and running with MEM. It's not the complete set of options (there are more than 100 different packages). If you need to evaluate which subscription your company should go with, I recommend you head to the Microsoft licensing page at https://bit.ly/37un2aS.

Do it – Create a new trial account

Follow these steps to get yourself a new MEM trial account that also contains other products we will use throughout this book:

1. Start a new InPrivate tab in your browser (I recommend this in case you are already signed into your browser somewhere with another organizational identity – you do not want to accidentally add a trial account to your company's tenant. Not yet anyway).

2. Use a search engine to search for "Microsoft EMS Trial" or use this short link (https://bit.ly/2PLZypq) to land on the subscription sign-up page and then choose "Free Trial".

3. Complete the online form with your contact details.

4. Choose a tenant name. Don't worry, for your lab environment the name doesn't need too much thought – later on, you can replace the ".onmicrosoft.com" domain name with a custom one.

5. Create an account and password for your administrator. Make a note of these credentials – you are going to need them in almost every exercise.

> **Tip! – What do the letters and numbers mean in subscription names like "E5"?**
>
> Microsoft subscriptions usually have a name like [ProductName][Industry][Size]. For example, Microsoft Office 365 E5 is the premium Office offering for enterprises. This cheat sheet should help you identify licenses from a subscription name:
>
> E = Enterprise, A = Education, G = Government, F = Firstline Worker
> 1 = Base Package, 3 = Medium Package, 5 = Premium Package

A quick tour of the MEM admin center

The Microsoft Endpoint Manager admin center is where (mostly) all the action happens and can be reached by using the URL https://endpoint.microsoft.com. As an Endpoint Manager ninja, you'll have this console open all the time. First, let's take a quick tour of the MEM admin center.

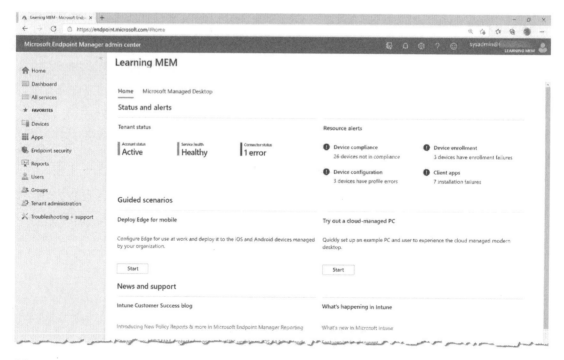

When you first log in to MEM you will hit a landing page that gives you a high-level picture of your tenant. Most of the data and visualizations on this page are going to be boring right now because you have not started managing devices or configured any policies.

The left-hand navigation menu provides some key options:

Devices

The Devices section is where you view all managed devices and create and deploy policies and profiles to them. You'll be using this part of the console a lot.

Apps

Here, you create and deploy applications to devices. You will also use this part of the console to deploy app-based policies and settings (both configuration and security types).

Endpoint security

This part is built specifically for endpoint security experts. It's a collection of all security-related functionality under one node. We'll drill into this in Chapter 7.

Reports

Reports is the destination for a collection of useful, pre-canned reports. We call the reports in this node "Organizational Reports" because they are intended to bubble up high-level organizational insights about your managed devices. For example, it contains a feature called Endpoint Analytics (EA) where you can visualize key business and technology metrics such as workstation boot time.

Users and groups

The Users and groups menu items are special. They are not like the other menu items in that they link you to features in Azure Active Directory (Azure AD). Because Endpoint Manager is tightly coupled with Azure AD for users and groups, when navigating to either of these in the menu you'll actually be looking at Azure AD console screens (we'll cover Azure AD in the next section). In your journey to be an Endpoint Manager ninja, you'll click on these a lot because you're going to need some new users and groups for testing it all out.

Tenant administration

This is where you will configure settings that impact your entire MEM tenant. Here, you'll configure connectors to other Microsoft or third-party services. This area is also where you configure role-based administration (RBAC).

Troubleshooting + support

A user calls the helpdesk with a problem with their device; where do you start? Well, right here! This navigation menu item is the starting point for troubleshooting any user or device issues. You can search for users in this blade, then enumerate all the devices, policies and apps that impact that user. Chapter 14 is dedicated to troubleshooting.

Do it – Take a tour of MEM

1. Log in to the MEM admin center (https://endpoint.microsoft.com)

2. Click through each of the navigation items on the left-hand menu (Home, Dashboard, Devices, Apps, Endpoint security, Reports, Users, Groups, Tenant administration, Troubleshooting + support.

Tip! – MEM Portal customization

You can customize your default MEM landing page and other admin center experiences like the theme, language, and notification settings using the "Portal settings" menu item. Just use the settings icon at the top right of the MEM admin center.

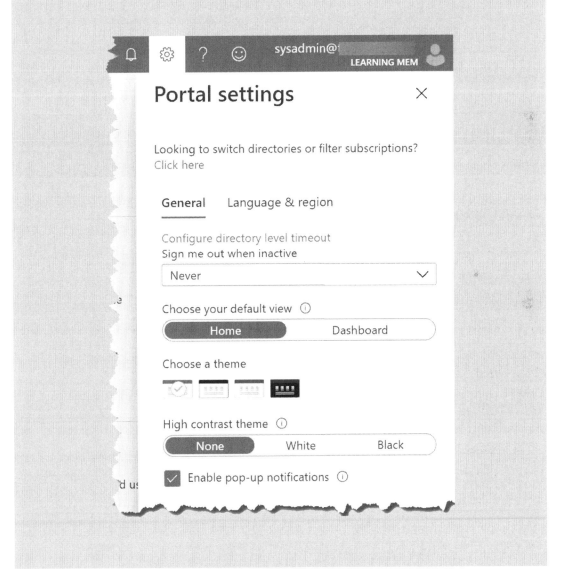

Azure Active Directory (Azure AD)

When you or your company starts a Microsoft subscription that includes MEM, you'll automatically be provisioned with an Azure AD tenant. Azure AD is the backbone directory of all Microsoft cloud services including MEM – it gets spun-up silently in the background during the setup process.

Amongst other things, Azure AD provides your organization with identity and access control services. As a MEM admin, the most important thing you should know is that Azure AD is where your user accounts and groups are stored. Even the devices you manage with MEM have a linked device object in Azure AD. If you are new to Azure AD, you will need to learn a few basic concepts before we hook into the juicy MEM content. In the next section, we'll go through how to create new user accounts in the cloud and assign them the licenses needed for MEM. Both tasks can be done from the MEM or Azure AD admin portal.

Creating cloud-only users

For all Microsoft cloud services, you need user accounts. In most existing organizations you would not actually need to create new users from scratch, it is much more likely that you would install a tool like Azure AD Connect on a server in your on-prem network that looks at your on-prem Active Directory users and syncs them (and their password hashes) into the cloud. The other option is to create "cloud-only" users, completely disconnected from any on-prem directory. This scenario is more likely for brand-new companies or startups that were born in the cloud and have no on-prem datacenters or directory. Since the goal of this book is to learn MEM, we'll put that complexity aside for now and create some "cloud-only" identities. We will cover connecting on-prem environments to the cloud in Chapter 12.

Custom domain name

New Azure AD tenants are always born with a *".onmicrosoft.com"* domain suffix. That means that all new users you create are going to have a username like *user@ comanyname.onmicrosoft.com* and would need to type that long username in whenever authenticating to an Azure AD-backed cloud service. While that might be ok for testing the exercises in this book, it is not going to fly in the real world. I recommend you take a quick detour at this point and head to a domain name registrar such as Go-Daddy.com. Find yourself a public internet domain name and then verify it in Azure AD (go to https://portal.azure.com > *Azure Active Directory* > *Custom domain names* > *Add custom domain*). My tip is to use a .xyz suffix because they are cheap – I paid around $2 for my last one. You can then apply that suffix by default to any new users you create.

In Chapter 12 we will cover connecting on-prem user accounts to Azure AD and at that point, you can map existing on-prem suffixes to this public domain suffix so that authentication across on-prem services and cloud services work seamlessly.

Do it – Create a new Azure AD user and assign licenses

Follow these steps to create your first user in MEM:

1. Go to the MEM admin center (https://endpoint.microsoft.com) and sign in using the admin username and password you created in the first exercise.
2. Choose *Users* from the left-hand navigation menu, then *New user*.
3. Add some fictitious user information and take note of the username and password.
4. Be sure to choose a usage location as this is needed to assign some licenses to the user.
5. After you successfully create the user, click on it and you will see more Azure AD configuration options in a left-hand menu.

6. Choose *Licenses*, then *Assignments*, and select one from the list of available licenses. The list should have the trial subscription you created in an earlier exercise.

7. Under *Review license options*, you should see *Microsoft Intune* listed and selected.

8. Choose *Save*. Your test user will now be properly licensed for MEM.

Tip! – Try out the Microsoft 365 admin center for creating users and assigning licenses

You can also create users and assign licenses in the Microsoft 365 admin center: https://admin.microsoft.com.

Tip! – Sync users from Active Directory using Azure AD Connect

It's not very practical in real-world organizations to manually create user accounts and assign licenses to them. The typical way that companies create user accounts is to integrate with other systems; for example, the human resources department already has a system for creating new users and populating all their employee information into the directory.

If your organization is still using on-prem systems (like Active Directory), typically these HR systems will be configured to create new Active Directory user accounts. To get these on-prem user accounts into the cloud so that you can start doing endpoint management, you will connect Active Directory to Azure AD with a tool called Azure AD Connect. Once users are synced into Azure AD you can assign licenses to the entire group. In Chapter 12 you will become more familiar with connecting AD to Azure AD with Azure AD Connect.

For steps on assigning licenses to a group instead of individual user accounts, see Microsoft docs: http://bit.ly/3ayEGMr.

Creating Azure AD groups

Groups are essential to MEM when it comes to targeting policies, apps and controlling access and administration. Like user accounts, groups in MEM are sourced from Azure AD. Within MEM admin center, the groups user interface (UI) itself is just a redirect to the Azure AD groups web page (which you can also see if you navigate to https://portal.azure.com and choose Azure Active Directory from the menu).

In MEM you will use groups for two main purposes:

- **Assignment** – When you create policies and apps (I'll refer to them generally as "workloads") in MEM, you need to assign them to devices or users. You can't assign workloads directly to individual devices or users; instead, you organize these devices into a group and then assign the workload to the group.

- **Role-based administration and control (RBAC)** – MEM allows you to control which set of admins has permissions to manage a given set of devices and workloads. If your organization is big enough that it needs to separate admins, then chances are that you'll be creating groups of admins for just this purpose.

MEM supports many of the Azure AD group types when it comes to assigning workloads or configuring RBAC. Groups can be security groups or Microsoft 365 groups and their members can either be manually populated with user and device objects or dynamically populated based on user or device properties.

Dynamic device groups are a very common group type used by MEM administrators. These groups allow you to define a set of criteria (in the form of device properties) so that devices are automatically placed into the right group as soon as they are enrolled. You can use the Azure AD dynamic group rule builder to put together over 14 different properties with expressions (like *Equals*, *Contains*, *Startswith*) and operators (like *And*, *Or*) to reach your desired result.

For example, if you have a goal to deploy a policy to all *corporate-owned Surface Pro devices* then you could create a dynamic group called "Corporate-owned Surface Pro devices" and build out a membership expression like this:

(device.deviceModel -contains "Surface Pro") and (device.deviceOwnership -eq "Company")

From now on, whenever a new corporate-owned Surface Pro device enrolls into MEM it will automatically get put into this group and receive any policy targeted at that dynamic group. A complete list of supported device properties for Azure AD dynamic groups can be found here: https://bit.ly/2Ftmp7v.

Do it – Create a user group

Follow these steps to create your first static group in the MEM admin center:

1. Go to the MEM admin center (https://endpoint.microsoft.com) and sign in.

2. On the left navigation menu choose *Groups* (Notice that this is the Azure AD groups blade embedded into the MEM admin center).

3. Select *New group*.

4. Make it a security group and add a name and description (I always use a real-world name like *HR Users*).

5. Under *Membership type*, select *Assigned*.

6. Under *Members*, choose the user you created in the last exercise.

7. After you select *Create*, you'll see a notification that your group was created; select it and you'll be able to view and edit the properties.

8. Now you have a group of users you can assign workloads to in MEM!

Do it – Create a dynamic user group

Follow these steps to create your first dynamic user group based on the user's country attribute:

1. Go to the MEM admin center (https://endpoint.microsoft.com) and sign in.

2. On the left navigation menu choose *Groups*.

3. Select *New group*.

4. Make it a security group based on country and add a name and description. My suggestion – Name: All Australian users, Description: This group is full of great people.

5. Under *Membership type*, select *Dynamic user*.

6. Select the *Add dynamic query* hyperlink under *Members*; you'll be taken to a dynamic group rule page.

7. Use the dropdown controls to craft a query that includes your users. My suggestion:

   ```
   (user.country -eq "Australia")
   ```

8. After you select *Create*, you'll see a notification that your group was created; select it and you'll be able to view and edit the properties and any members that were added.

9. If you used my suggested properties, then there is a good chance that the group membership is empty. Head back to the *Users* page and update the Country property of the user account you created. Give it some time – dynamic group calculation is not instant.

10. Now you should see members being populated in the group. Well done!

Tip! – You can create nested groups!

It's possible to nest security groups within other groups if that makes your admin role a little easier. For example, you could have "HR Department global group" and its members could be "HR Department US" "HR Department APAC" and "HR Department EMEA". In MEM you could assign a workload to the global parent group rather than each region individually.

Management choices – Mobile Device Management (MDM) and Mobile Application Management (MAM)

MEM provides you with flexible options for securing and controlling data on corporate devices. In some scenarios you might need to apply more rigid device controls and restrictions but in others you might get away with lighter (and more user-friendly) management that still achieves the right data protection outcomes. In this section we will cover the differences between Mobile Device Management (MDM) and Mobile Application Management (MAM).

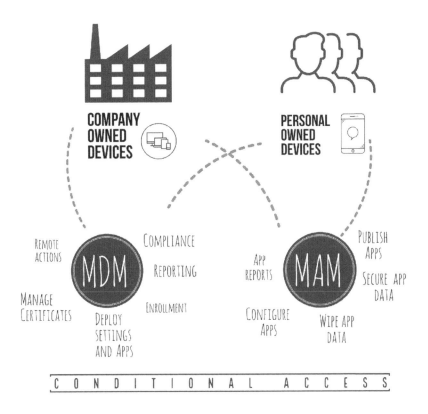

Mobile Device Management (MDM)

Microsoft Endpoint Manager is known to most people as a "Mobile Device Management" (MDM) product. Up until around 2019, MDM was the industry term used by people when talking about controlling apps and configuration of mobile devices (originally just mobile phones but gradually used for laptops too). More recently, the professionals who work in this area have used the term "Unified Endpoint Management" (UEM). This change reflects the shift in the industry where management products such as MEM became unified product suites used to manage a much larger set of endpoints than just mobile devices. For example, MEM (through integration with Configuration Manager) is used to manage a huge amount of desktop PC's but also has some capabilities managing servers.

Industry terminology aside, "MDM" is still the term we use across all platforms when we talk about "enrollment". Before you can manage an iPhone, you need it to enroll in "MDM". For Windows, setting configuration can come from either Group Policy (like in the old days) or via MDM. Each platform's operating system has a built-in "MDM Stack" whose job it is to accept incoming MDM commands (from Intune or any other modern management product) and then make that change happen on the device. Let's discuss how this MDM stack works on different platforms:

iOS/iPadOS

MEM handles managed iOS and iPadOS devices in a similar way. There is a high overlap in available configuration settings and apps for both. The MDM stack on iOS and iPadOS has a lot of flexibility when it comes to enrollment. Corporate-owned iPhones and iPads can be enrolled in an automated way via Apple's Automated Device Enrollment (ADE) (also known as Device Enrollment Program (DEP)) or devices can be enrolled manually by the end-users themselves. We will cover the specifics of Apple enrollment in Chapter 3.

Apple also implements a concept known as "Supervision" in the MDM stack. To fully control and manage every setting available through the MDM, the device first needs to be set into "Supervised-mode". Within MEM, you can easily tell which devices are in this mode and which settings are available only to devices in this mode.

macOS

You can enroll Macs into MEM, too. The options for enrollment and management are similar, but not as comprehensive as iOS and iPadOS. In addition to supporting apps and policies, the macOS platform has the advantage of being able to receive customization profiles via admin-created bash scripts containing any desired configuration.

Android

Android is a complex beast and a fast-moving target for MEM and other UEM products to keep up with. Before I go into any detail, first a history lesson:

Android device administrator (Also known as Android DA or Android legacy management)

Early Android device management (since version 2.2) did not really have an "MDM Stack". Instead, the Android operating system shipped to devices with a "Device Admin API". UEM products like MEM built their own device management apps and hosted them in the Android app store. The apps, once installed, interact with the device (to configure settings) via the device admin API. For MEM, this app is the "Company Portal" app. In this "Android DA" mode of management, the Company Portal app gets installed by an end-user who would have to manually grant the app permission to be a Device Administrator in settings so the app can receive management commands from the UEM product and then interact directly with the OS to apply those settings. This older management mode is still used by many companies today, mainly for devices that don't support the newer Android Enterprise MDM stack or for companies that enrolled devices with this method and never migrated away. Google officially deprecated this mode starting with Android 10.0.

Android Enterprise

Starting with Android 5.0, Google started introducing new mobile device management capabilities and architecture for Android. The model, originally called "Android for Work" but later renamed to Android Enterprise, divided Android device management into four modes that line up with ownership:

Work profile

- **Personal devices with work profile** – This method is best used to manage personal devices in bring your own device (BYOD) scenarios. When a device is enrolled in this method of management, the device is conceptually divided into two partitions – a personal partition and a corporate partition. Data is not allowed to transfer between the partitions and because this is a BYOD device, admins have a limited level of control over the device itself. For example, admins are restricted so that they cannot remotely wipe the entire device, only the corporate partition that contains company-owned data and applications.

Dedicated devices

- **Corporate-owned dedicated devices** (formerly known as Corporate-Owned/ Single-Use (COSU)) – This management profile is used in Kiosk scenarios and task-based devices. If you need to manage a digital sign or a Point-of-Sale (POS) terminal or scanner, you will likely use this mode.

- **Corporate-owned device with work profile devices** (formerly known as Corporate-Owned/Personally enabled (COPE)) – This management mode is used for devices bought and supplied to users by their company. The intent of this mode is that the organization owns the device, so they should be allowed to do what they want to it, but still allow the user to have a partition to host their personal apps and settings. As an admin you can expect a good range of management capabilities as well as benefit from one of Google's corporate device enrollment methods such as Zero Touch.

- **Corporate-owned, fully managed user devices** (formerly known as Corporate-Owned/Business-Only (COBO)) – COBO is for devices that are 100% owned by the company and used only for work reasons. Users are prevented from accessing some features of the device such as resetting the device from settings.

Windows 10

The only rival to Android's management complexity is Windows 10. There is just so much history to unpack.

For the last 20-ish years, companies used two main methods to manage Windows PC's: Group Policy and/or Microsoft Configuration Manager. Yes, there were exceptions (I was once a Novell Netware administrator), and Configuration Manager certainly had competitor products at the enterprise level, but these tools were the most common. Under the hood, the thing that enabled management of PC's was either an installed agent (in the case of Configuration Manager) or the Windows built-in "Group Policy stack" (Group Policy engine, configuration service providers etc.).

Around the Windows 8.1 and Windows Phone timeframe, with massive swings to laptops and mobility, Microsoft began introducing a new built-in management stack for MDM. Now, with the addition of this new management stack, enterprise configuration on devices could be achieved in a new way – and via the internet, they no longer had to be within line-of-sight to a domain controller to receive group policy or a Configuration Manager server to install apps.

With this new management stack, Windows devices, once enrolled into MDM, can check in regularly over the internet with their MDM server and receive the latest configuration and policies. Nowadays, all new Windows 10 settings can be controlled using MDM first – some don't even get enabled for group policy and must always be flipped using MDM.

An overview of Mobile Application Management (MAM)

Mobile Application Management (MAM) is another overloaded term in the industry. Over the years the term has been used generally when talking about any aspect of app management. Deploying an app to a set of users on their mobile devices, configuring that app with an enterprise-specific configuration setting or applying security settings to it are all considered MAM. In MEM you will hear people talking about MAM in the last way – the security type. This is because Microsoft first came out with the security type and later re-branded it to "app protection policies".

App protection policies (APP)

App protection policies (APP's) are an especially important part of the product and extremely useful if you need to manage iOS or Android mobile devices. APP's are a set of security-based settings that you can configure on mobile applications. These rules are to protect app security and secure enterprise data as workers use the mobile apps across both corporate and personal devices. For example, you could configure an APP policy so that when users in your organization install the Outlook mobile app on their personal phones (which do not have to be enrolled into MDM, by the way), the users must set a PIN for the Outlook app. That way, you can ensure all the app's data is encrypted. The policy could also enforce that users are not allowed to save or export any of the data from the Outlook app into other personal apps that are not encrypted.

When using app protection policies, you don't need to enroll devices into MDM. You can, if you want to configure the devices in other ways, but you don't need to. This is one of the reasons APP is so popular – because in many organizations, users are increasingly fighting back against their organization and IT department when asked to enroll their own personal devices into management. IT departments are in a tough position – on one hand they need to protect the company's data and on the other they need to keep their users happy and willing to use the productivity tools provided. APP works great because of its lightweight setup process tied to the user's company login. It can be used for all the major Microsoft first-party productivity apps (Outlook mobile, Word, Excel, PowerPoint, OneDrive, Teams and more) in addition to third-party apps like Zoom and ServiceNow. Companies can also integrate an Intune APP SDK or an app-wrapping tool to make these APP settings available within their own line-of-business (LOB) company apps.

Tip! – A note on app protection policies for Windows 10

Windows 10 also supports a form of app protection policies (APP), but it works completely differently to the iOS and Android flavor that I talk about in this book. The Windows 10 platform itself comes with a technology called Windows Information Protection (WIP) where admins can define app security settings in a similar way to APP. It has some very powerful features – for example, admins can define a set of "Corporate" boundaries in the form of cloud services (e.g., SharePoint Online) or networks (domains, subnets, proxy servers etc.) and then anything that comes from those locations is treated as "Corporate" data. You can make sure data is encrypted and there is a workflow where if the device is removed from management (for example, the user gets fired or loses it on a night out), the encryption key will be revoked and the data rendered unusable. Probably the biggest difference for Windows 10 when compared to iOS and Android app protection is that you can use it across any apps – so apps don't need to have been developed using the Intune APP SDK.

CHAPTER 3

ENROLLING DEVICES INTO MANAGEMENT

Roll up your sleeves, this is where the real fun begins! In this chapter we will dive into device enrollment. You will learn how to get devices under management, showing up in the MEM admin center and put into groups so that you can start managing them.

Introduction to enrollment

Before you can get to work configuring devices and deploying apps, you will first need to set up enrollment into device management. The enrollment setup tasks are generally quick and easy but there are a few gotchas along the way. The key thing to learn in this chapter is the various "modes" of management that a device enrolls in, because once it is enrolled it is stuck like this (until you factory reset it and try again, that is). The method you choose for enrollment has a direct relationship with the "mode" of management for the device and can have consequences down the track when it comes to things you can do to the device, so you'll need to take that into consideration and not just choose the most convenient method available.

Getting started with Apple enrollment

There are a bunch of different options available when it comes to enrolling Apple devices and it can sometimes be confusing deciding which to use. Here, I will break down all the mumbo-jumbo and have you 'doing it' as quickly as possible.

Before we get too far into the details and nuances of Apple enrollment types, we should cover the general prerequisite for enrollment. This is a good time to point out that you are going to need something called an "Apple MDM Push Certificate" (also known as an APNs (Apple Push Notification Service certificate)) to enroll any Apple device (iPad, iPhone, MacBook) into management.

The push certificate allows MDM products like MEM to establish a connection between Apple and MEM services. For example, when you issue a "Remote wipe" command to a device under management, MEM would send a command to Apple who invoke their Apple Push Notification service (APNs) to push a command to the device so that it can wake up and get wiped.

The good news is that the setup process is straightforward and free. All you need is a valid Apple ID.

Tip! – Don't use your own Apple ID for your company's Apple Push Certificate

If you're setting up MEM for your company it is important that you create a new Apple ID to use just for MEM. Remember, this certificate expires every 12 months and can only be renewed by logging back in with that Apple ID. I have heard horror stories about companies that set up MDM using an administrator's personal Apple ID, only to have that admin leave the company. The result was that all devices needed to be re-enrolled into management. Ouch!

Do it – Set up Apple Push Certificate

1. Go to the Apple website (https://appleid.apple.com/account) and create a new Apple ID. If you are setting this up on behalf of your company, make sure this is a generic account for your organization. DO NOT use your own personal information here and don't turn on two-factor authentication for your own mobile phone. Re-

member, this will be used long after you move on to your next Endpoint Manager Rockstar position.

2. Head back into the MEM admin center (https://endpoint.microsoft.com) and sign in.

3. Select *Devices, Enroll devices, Apple enrollment* then *Apple MDM Push Certificate*.

4. In the context pane that opens, walk through the five-step process.

   a. Agree to terms.

   b. Download the certificate signing request (.csr) file. It doesn't matter what you name it or where you place it, just keep it handy for the next step.

   c. Follow the link to the Apple APN portal, sign in with your newly created account, accept terms and choose *Create certificate*.

   d. Make sure to include notes. Notes are handy for renewing certificates later down the track, particularly if you've accumulated more than one after testing multiple MDM products or maintaining multiple lab environments. I suggest something like "Scott is creating this push certificate for use with Microsoft Endpoint Manager as part of Endpoint Manager POC project".

   e. Under *Choose file*, grab the .csr file that you exported from MEM and then select *Upload*.

   f. If all worked well, *Download* the certificate file with a .pem extension.

   g. Return to MEM and complete the process by entering your Apple ID and uploading the certificate.

> **Tip! – Don't let your APNs certificate expire!**
>
> Put a note in your calendar to renew the certificate 12 months from now! If your endpoint management team shares a calendar put it in that! The more people that are alerted the better. MEM will notify you of expiring APNS certificates but if you're not in the console on a daily basis you could miss it. If that certificate expires you'll be in a world of hurt. I'm talking mass device re-enrollment.

Now that we have MEM set up to start enrolling Apple devices, let's look at the various enrollment methods. At a high level, the enrollment methods are broken down into two categories: Personal devices and Corporate-owned devices. We'll cover personal enrollment first.

Apple enrollment for personal devices

To enroll personal device into MEM, you'll ask end-users to walk through the device enrollment process on their own devices. The setup flow starts with the user downloading the MEM "Company Portal" app from the app store and then being guided through the process. First they'll sign in and then download and approve a management profile.

Do it – Enroll an iOS device into MDM

1. Make sure you've completed the last exercise to set up an Apple push certificate.
2. On your test iOS device (iPad or iPhone), go to the App Store and search for "Company Portal". Once you find the right app (the one published by Microsoft), go ahead and download it.
3. Open the app and sign in with a test user account (use the one you created in Chapter 1).
4. Once signed-in you'll be prompted to "Set up access" and be guided through a four-step MDM enrolment process. In this process you'll be prompted to download an MDM profile, then directed to the settings app where you'll need to install it.

5. After installing the MDM profile, return to the Company Portal app to finish the enrollment process.

6. Go back to the MEM admin center, then to *Devices > All devices* and you will see the device you just enrolled.

Tip! – User enrollment for iOS and iPadOS

In 2019 Apple released a new variant for enrolling personal iOS devices called "User enrollment". The concept is that this enrollment method provides users with a better promise on privacy and control by restricting many of the MDM actions that can be performed on the device. For example, when a device is "User enrolled" you can't initiate a device wipe on it from the MEM admin center.

MEM distinguishes between the two types of personal device enrollment as "User enrollment" and "Device enrollment" and as the IT person, you can choose which route your devices go down. At the time of writing this book, User enrollment is a preview feature.

Apple enrollment for corporate devices

Use one of these methods to enroll corporate devices into MEM:

Apple's Automated Device Enrollment (ADE)

Most people know this method as Apple DEP (Device Enrollment Program). The concept is that iOS, iPadOS and macOS devices can all be individually pre-registered for your organization (and your MEM tenant) at the time of purchase. This means when it comes time to set them up, it will be super-fast and efficient. When you power them on, they'll only need to be connected to the internet and need minimum interaction to be enrolled and start getting the configuration you've defined in MEM.

Apple Configurator

One of the oldest ways to enroll devices is to use Apple Configurator. Apple Configurator is an application that only runs on macOS computers (so if you want to try it out you might need to trade in your PC). With this method, you must manually connect iPhones or iPads directly with a lightning cable to your Mac running Apple Configurator. Once the device is connected you can directly apply settings that you have configured in an Apple Configurator profile, including direct enrollment settings. Due to the amount of touch that devices require, I consider this enrollment method as a last resort. Use it in cases where DEP isn't available.

Supervised mode

I think of Apple's "Supervised" mode as "god" mode. When you put your managed devices into this mode, you can manage everything – all the settings you need to get the job done. Within the MEM admin center, it is easy to see which settings depend on supervision as you'll see a "Supervised" tag next to the setting name. How do you get devices into "Supervised" mode? Generally, this is only done using Apple's Automated Device Enrollment program and selecting the option to supervise devices. There is one other (labor intensive) way though: you can connect apple devices directly to a macOS device via lightning cable and use a program called Apple Configurator 2 to enable it.

> **Tip! – Supervised mode settings**
>
> For a complete reference of settings, I recommend reading (and bookmarking) this Apple documentation (https://apple.co/2CHgTgr).

Do it – Set up and enroll devices with ADE

This is a three-part exercise:

- Part 1 – Set up the connection between MEM and Apple Business Manager or Apple School Manager.

- Part 2 – Create an ADE profile and assign it to iOS devices to be used as userless kiosk devices.

- Part 3 – Walk through automated enrollment on the device.

Note: This exercise requires you to have an existing Apple Business Manager (ABM) or Apple School Manager (ASM) account. If your organization does not have one of these yet you will first need to create one at https://business.apple.com/#enrollment. To create an ABM or ASM account you must provide Apple with your organizations D-U-N-S number which proves you are an authorized organization. If you do not have one of these, then follow the links on the Apple create page to create one.

Part 1 – Set up Apple Enrollment Program connector.

1. Go to the MEM admin center (https://endpoint.microsoft.com) and sign in. Navigate to *Devices > Enroll devices*.

2. Select *Apple enrollment*, then *Enrollment program tokens*. Then select *Add*.

3. Follow each of the steps in the wizard; download your public key (in .pem format) from MEM and save it locally.

4. Follow the link to the Apple Business Manager or Apple School Manager portal and sign in using your Apple credentials. Keep the MEM web page open in a separate browser tab as you will return here shortly.

5. Once signed into Apple Business Manager, go to *Settings* and under *Device Management Settings* select *Add MDM Server*.

6. Add a descriptive MDM Server name such as "Microsoft Endpoint Manager" for the new MDM server.

7. Select *Choose file* to upload the .pem file you exported from the MEM admin center.

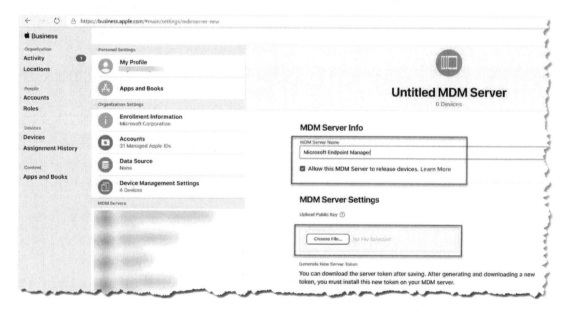

8. After the MDM Server is created, select *Download Token*. A token in .P7m format will be downloaded locally.

9. Optionally, select *Change default device assignment* to ensure all new devices coming into ABM or ASM are assigned to this (Microsoft Endpoint Manager) MDM server.

10. Now go to the *Devices* menu. You will see devices that were purchased by your company through the ADE program. Choose *Edit device management* for one or more devices and then assign to the MDM server you just created.

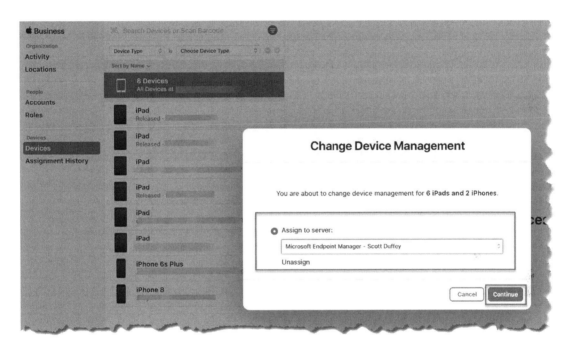

Tip! – Don't have any devices yet? No worries!

If you don't have any devices registered into your ABM or ASM account yet to assign to MEM, you can manually register them using Apple Configurator 2 – skip ahead to the "Try it – manually register devices" section below and then come back here to assign them.

11. Return to the MEM admin center enrollment program setup page, type the Apple ID that you used to create the token and upload the token.

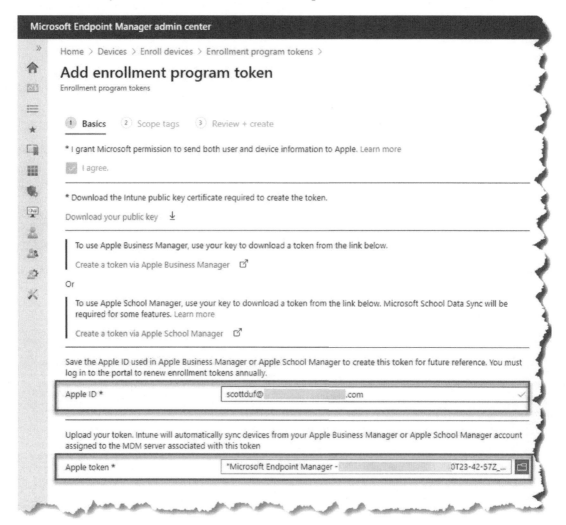

12. Complete the setup wizard and select *Create*. Now all devices that were assigned in ABM or ASM will automatically be synced to MEM and appear under the *Devices* menu item under the token name.

Part 2 – Create an Apple Automated Device profile and assign it.

1. While still in MEM, within the context of the ADE token connection you just established, select *Profiles* from the navigation menu, then *Create profile*.

2. Choose a suitable profile name – for example, *My supervised kiosk iPads*

3. On the *Management Settings* screen, select the following options:

   a. User affinity: Enroll without User affinity

   b. Supervised: Yes

   c. Locked enrollment: No

   d. Shared iPad: No

   e. Sync with computers: Allow all

   f. Apply Device name template: No

Tip! – Apply device name templates

In the real world it is a good idea to apply a device name template – otherwise, your devices will get the default name of "iPhone" or "iPad" and they will all look the same in the MEM admin center. As a bonus step in this exercise, try using the {{Serial}} and/or the {{DeviceType}} variables.

Device Name

Apply device name template (supervised only) ⓘ   [Yes] No

Variables supported: {{SERIAL}}, {{DEVICETYPE}}

Device Name Template: ⓘ   Shareddevice-{{SERIAL}}   ✓

---

4. On the setup assistant screen, add a department (e.g., My test department) and a dummy phone number. These are both required fields.

5. Toggle all screens to *Hide* to reduce the setup steps needed.

6. Review the configuration and then select *Create*.

7. Now click on the profile and select *Assign devices*, then *Add devices*. Choose the device with the serial number that matches your test device.

Part 3 – Walk through automated enrollment on the device.

1. Turn on your test iOS device. Select the language and region. You may also need to connect to a Wi-Fi network if your device doesn't have mobile data.

2. On the *Remote Management* screen choose *Next*. The device will now connect with Apple and apply the appropriate enrollment profile that was assigned in MEM.

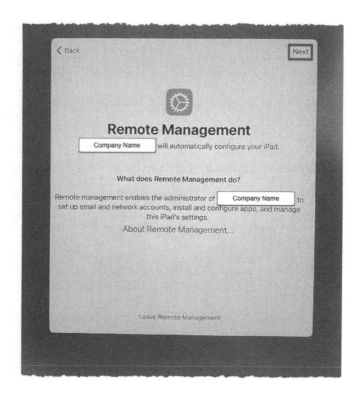

3. Notice that the device skips all the remaining setup screens and lands directly at the home screen.

4. Go to *Settings* and notice the message *This device is supervised and managed by…* at the top left.

5. Return to the MEM admin center and then select *Devices > iOS/iPadOS devices*. Notice that your test device now shows in the list.

6. Select *Columns* from the top menu and add the *Supervised* column and you can see that the device has a *Supervised* value of *Yes*.

7. Optionally, create a few more Apple enrollment profiles that you might find useful for other scenarios used in your organization. At a minimum I recommend trying a profile that establishes *User Device Affinity* during the setup process.

Do it – Manually register iOS devices into ABM with Apple Configurator 2

If you don't have any devices showing up in Apple Business Manager (ABM) it could be because you haven't bought any through the ADE program yet. Don't worry, you can manually register them. All you need is a macOS device running the Apple Configurator 2 app and the physical iOS iPhone or iPad that you want to register. Here are the steps:

Before you start, make sure the test device is not locked to any personal Apple ID. If it is, the registration will fail.

1. On a macOS device, install the Apple Configurator 2 application from the App Store.

2. Using a lightning cable, connect the test device to your Mac and then open the Apple Configurator 2 app.

3. **This step is needed if you are using a test device without its own data con-nection** – Go to *File > New profile > Wi-Fi > Configure* and add the minimum Wi-Fi connection details needed to allow the device to connect to Wi-Fi during its registration process. On my home network this is simply the SSID and the WPA2 password. Go to *File > Save* to save it to your local drive – you will need it in an upcoming step.

4. Select *Prepare* from the menu at the top of the screen.

5. On the *Prepare Devices* screen ensure the following options are set and then select *Next*.

   a. Prepare with: Manual enrollment.

   b. Add to Apple School Manager or Apple Business Manager: checked.

   c. All other options are not needed for this exercise and can remain unchecked.

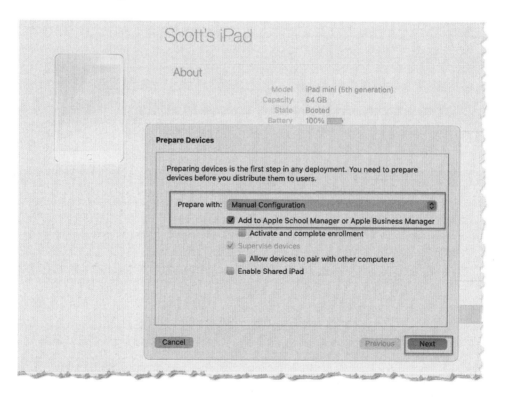

6. On the *Enroll in MDM Server* page, leave the default option of *New server* and then choose *Next*.

7. On the *Define and MDM Server* page, type a friendly name such as *Microsoft Endpoint Manager*.

To populate the *Host name or URL* field on this page you will copy and paste the URL from the MEM admin center by first generating an Apple Configurator profile. You won't be using this for enrollment – just using it to find the URL.

8. Open the MEM admin center and go to *Devices > Enroll Devices > Apple enrollment > Apple Configurator > Profiles > Create*. Add a name such as "Test AC Profile" and, on the *Settings* page, choose *Enroll without user affinity* and the complete the wizard.

9. Once the configuration profile is created, select it and choose *Export profile*. Copy the *Profile URL* from the context pane that opens and paste it into Apple Configurator.

10. If you receive an error *Unable to verify the MDM server URL* you can safely ignore it and select *Next*.

11. On the *Trust Anchor* page, select *Manage.microsoft.com* from the list and then select *Next*.

12. On the *Sign-in to ASM or ABM* screen, provide your ASM/ABM sign-in credentials.

13. On the *Create Organization* screen select *Generate a supervision identity*.

14. On the *Setup Assistant* screen, select *Don't show any of these steps*.

15. On the *Network* screen, select the Wi-Fi profile that you created.

16. On the same screen, select *Choose* and then locate the Wi-Fi profile that you created earlier. If your test device has a data connection, you can leave this blank.

17. Select *Prepare*. You will be prompted for the admin credentials of the local macOS device.

18. The test device will now go through each of the steps to prepare and register into ABM /ASM. Once it completes, sign in to ABM and check for the device by its serial number.

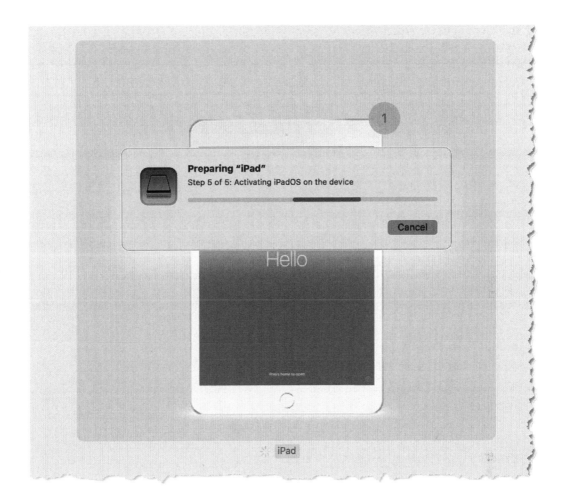

Do it – Set up a device using Apple Configurator

If you do not have access to an Apple Business Manager (ABM) or Apple School Manager (ASM) account, you can still test out device settings that require supervision, but you will first need to enroll the device using Apple Configurator (AC). The process involves connecting an iOS test device directly to a macOS device via lightning cable and preparing it using the Apple Configurator 2 app. From there you can manually configure the device into Supervised mode via an Apple Configurator profile in MEM. The three parts to this exercise are:

- Part 1 – Create an Apple Configurator Profile

- Part 2 – Prepare the device using Apple Configurator

- Part 3 – Enroll the device

Part 1 – Create the Apple Configurator Profile.

1. In the MEM admin center, go to *Device > Enroll Devices> Apple enrollment, then Apple Configurator*.

2. Go to *Profiles then* Select *Create*.

3. On the *basics* screen, provide a name and description (e.g., Supervised Mode AC Profile). Select *Next*.

4. On the *Settings* screen, choose *Enroll with User Affinity* and accept the default option of using the *Company Portal* for user authentication.

Tip! – If you use Azure AD Multi-factor authentication you should use the Company Portal authentication option

One of the first issues I worked on when helping customers with iOS deployment was this issue with ADE and AC enrollments. The problem was that the Apple Setup Assistant screen (aka OOBE) doesn't support modern authentication and Multi-factor authentication (MFA) – there was no way to show the Azure AD MFA screen during the setup screens which blocked any MFA-enabled user accounts from setting up devices. Thankfully, MEM introduced a change where the user authentication step could be moved from the initial setup assistant screens to further in the process, once the Company Portal app (which supports modern authentication and MFA) has been installed.

5. Complete the steps to create the Apple Configurator profile, then go to the devices page.

6. Select *Add*.

7. To add devices, first create a list of them in a .csv file format and upload that list in the *Add devices* context pane. To create a list, open a text editor (such as notepad) and list devices in the format of "<Serial number>,<device details>".

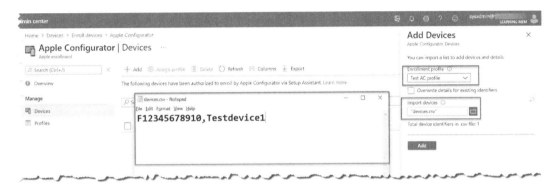

8. Choose the enrollment profile that you just created and then select *Add*.

Part 2 – Prepare the device using Apple Configurator.

1. On your admin macOS device, install the Apple Configurator 2 app from the App Store.

2. Using a lightning cable, connect the test device to your Mac and then open the Apple Configurator 2 app.

3. Select *Prepare* from the menu at the top of the screen.

4. On the *Prepare Devices* screen ensure the following options are set and then select *Next*.

   a. Prepare with: Manual enrollment

   b. Add to Apple School Manager or Apple Business Manager: unchecked

   c.   Supervise devices: checked

   d.   Allow devices to pair with other computers: checked

   e.   Enable shared iPad: unchecked

5.   On the *Enroll in MDM Server* page, choose the *Microsoft Endpoint Manager* MDM server you created in the last exercise – if you don't have that available, select *New Server* and then choose *Next*.

6.   On the *Define an MDM Server* page, type a friendly name such as *Microsoft Endpoint Manager*.

7.   To populate the *Host name or URL* field you will copy and paste the URL from the MEM admin center. In the MEM admin center open the Apple Configurator profile and select *Export profile*.

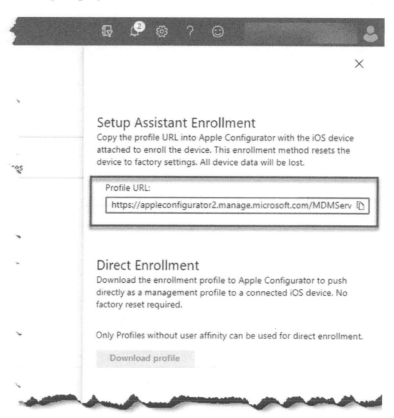

8. Copy the *Profile URL* from the context pane that opens and paste it into Apple Configurator.

9. If you receive an error *Unable to verify the MDM server URL* you can safely ignore it and select *Next*.

10. On the *Trust Anchor* page, select *appleconfigurator2.Manage.microsoft.com* from the list and then select *Next*.

11. On the *Sign in to ASM or ABM* screen, select *Skip*.

12. On the *Create Organization* screen, type some basic details about your tenant and then choose *Next*.

13. Select *Generate a new supervision identity*.

14. On the *Setup Assistant* screen, select *Don't show any of these steps*. Then select *Next*.

15. You will be prompted for your local macOS credentials at this point so that Apple Configurator can access the keychain. Type your username and password and then choose *Update settings*. If the test device is in a prepared state already it will prompt you to erase the device first.

16. When the preparation process completes, the test device will be ready and waiting for setup at the *Hello* screen. At this point you can disconnect it from your Mac and walk through an automated enrollment.

Part 3 – Enroll the device.

17. Start setting up the device – on the *Choose a Wi-Fi network* screen, add the Wi-Fi network details so that the device can connect to MEM over the internet. If your device has a mobile data connection, you may skip this screen.

18. On the *Remote Management* page, select *Apply configuration*. The setup process will proceed without any additional screens. At the end of the process, the device will be enrolled into MEM.

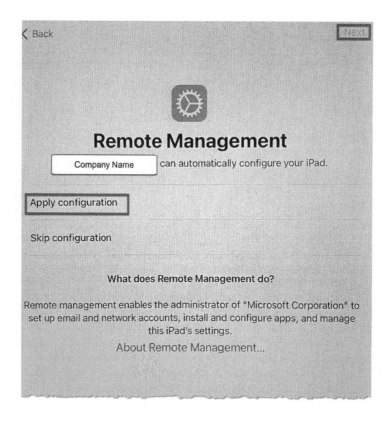

19. After you are logged in, you will see a device prompt to sign in with choices to *Use an existing Apple ID* or *Create a new Apple ID*. This sign-in is needed so that you can download the Company Portal app from the App Store.

20. If you have a test Apple ID, sign in with it, otherwise create a new one.

21. When the Company Portal app is installed, open it, sign in and complete the setup steps.

22. Return to the MEM admin center *Devices > All devices* and you will see the device is enrolled in MEM.

Getting started with Android enrollment

When it comes to enrolling Android devices, you have quite a few choices. Those choices really come down to what sort of devices you are trying to enroll. Are you enrolling mobile phones or are you trying to set up an Android-based barcode scanner?

MEM supports enrollment into four key Android Enterprise usage scenarios:

- Android Enterprise work profile (also known as Android for Work)

- Android Enterprise dedicated (also known as COSU)

- Android Enterprise fully managed (also known as COBO)

- Android Enterprise corporate-owned with work profile (Also known as COPE)

These usage scenarios will have a lot to do with the way you enroll devices. For example, the process of setting up a hundred new Zebra devices to be barcode scanners in a new location retail store needs to be highly automated and optimized but the process for a single user to set up their own mobile phone for work usage should be familiar and adaptable to meet your end-user's needs. More information about Google's Android Enterprise program can be found on the Google documentation page: https://bit.ly/31lVx1L.

PERSONAL DEVICES   COMPANY DEVICES

WORK PROFILE   DEDICATED   FULLY MANAGED   CORP OWNED WORK PROFILE

BYOD   KIOSK / DIGITAL SIGNS   WORK USAGE   WORK AND PERSONAL USAGE

SCOTT DUFFEY

Tip! – Android Device Administrator (DA)

Technically, there are five Android usage scenarios if you count Android Device Administrator (DA). Google started deprecating the API's used in this method in Android 9.0 and continue to turn off management functionality with each OS release. Organizations are actively migrating away from it, so it will not be covered in this book.

No matter how you plan to use the enrolled Android devices, you will need to create a Google account and register a new organization with Android Enterprise services. This setup is key to Android Enterprise management. Devices working in this mode of management can communicate directly with Google Management Service (GMS). The architecture is such that MEM's job is to create policies and tell GMS about them and which devices should get those policies – GMS does the rest.

Tip! – Check Android Enterprise region support

Make sure Android Enterprise is supported by Google to work in the regions you will be deploying devices. If there is no access to Google Management Services (GMS), devices will not be able to enroll or check in. One key callout is that Android Enterprise cannot be used in China. See the current list here: https://bit.ly/34gX7DL

Do it – Set up Android Enterprise and connect it to MEM

1. Go to the MEM admin center (https://endpoint.microsoft.com) and sign in.

2. On the left navigation menu choose *Device, Android* and then *Android enrollment*.

3. Select *Managed Google Play: Link your managed Google Play account to Intune*.

4. Check the box to grant permission to link the services, then select *Launch Google to connect now*.

5. A new browser page will open for you to link the accounts. Notice that the URL contains some token information that tells google which Intune tenant to connect to.

6. On the new browser page, choose *Sign in*. At this point you can create a new Google account for your organization to use. I'll say it again – if you are setting this up for your company, DO NOT USE your own Google account. Create a new one explicitly for the purpose of device management.

7. Once successfully signed in, choose *Get started*. On the next screen you need to add a name to identify this instance of Android Enterprise and notice that *Intune* is already populated in the MEM provider field.

8. On the next privacy page, you'll need to agree to Google's terms and optionally provide details for your company's privacy contacts.

9. Choose *Complete setup* and you are done. You'll be returned to the MEM admin center and you'll see a message saying the connector is set up.

Tip! – Create a Google account for your company

When you create a new Google account, do not sign in with your own personal Google account if you have one. Instead, create a new account for device management – when you create it you can also choose the option, *To manage my business*, instead of a personal account.

Android enrollment for personal devices

Only one of the four Android Enterprise management profiles discussed earlier is used specifically for personal or BYOD (bring your own device) scenarios. The Android Enterprise work profile (aka Android for Work) was the first one released by Google and supported in MEM. To get devices into this mode of management you'll have users enroll themselves from the Company Portal app.

Personal device enrollment with the Endpoint Manager Company Portal app

To enable bring your own device (BYOD) scenarios for Android in your organization, you will most likely want to enable "work profile". Before you rush out and set it up, there is one key consideration: do you need to enroll devices into MDM at all? In many companies, app protection policies can offer enough data protection and management capabilities in a more efficient and lightweight manner. Make sure you look at Chapter 7 – App Protection Policies.

So, what is "work profile" and why is it good for BYOD scenarios? The concept is that the Android device belongs to the user and has the user's personal stuff on it (emails, texts, apps at cat videos) and therefore the work stuff (email, apps, documents etc.) should not interfere with that at all. On top of that, the work stuff needs to be encrypted. In addition, IT admins should have a super-limited view of the personal stuff and no access to initiate any destructive remote actions. This is a huge improvement over the legacy Android DA style of management. I've heard horror stories of users losing their entire collection of cat photos due to a malicious or clumsy IT pro who was doing "clean ups" in the MEM admin center. With work profile, this can't happen – a portion of the phone is carved out to host the enterprise data and that "work profile" is where Endpoint Manager is allowed to enact management tasks like delivering apps and policies.

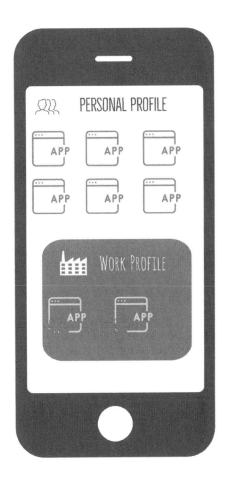

The user experience for enrolling into work profile is straightforward. To start the process, users are directed to go to the Google Play Store on their device and find the Company Portal app. The Company Portal app guides the user through the two-step process; first a work profile partition is created, then the user is guided through enrolling into it. After enrolling, users will notice that they now have duplicate app icons – the apps delivered by endpoint manager have a briefcase icon on them and their personal apps don't.

Tip! – Posters!

Most organizations I have worked with over the years found creative ways to help users enroll their phones into management. One great idea that works for all scenarios where you ask users to enroll their own devices is to print out posters or send emails. Put the posters up around the office and you will see a big uptick in enrollment. Microsoft provides some customizable samples in the Intune Adoption Kit: http://bit. ly/36F5fys.

Do it – Enroll into Android Enterprise work profile

1. Go to the MEM admin center (https://endpoint.microsoft.com) and sign in.

2. Make sure Android Enterprise (work profile) is an allowed form of enrollment. Go to *Devices > Enroll devices*, then select the (default) Device type restriction policy. Under *Properties* you should see a summary of the types that are allowed. The important thing is to make sure that Android Enterprise (work profile) is set to *Allow*.

Tip! – Android DA vs Android work profile in Enrollment Restrictions

You can use Enrollment Restriction policies to configure how you want personal device enrollment to happen. If you only want devices enrolled into work profile, then you should explicitly block Android device administrator. If both policies are set to *Allow*, devices will prefer to enroll into work profile. If those devices don't support work profile, they'll be allowed to enroll in Android device administrator. More details on the Microsoft docs page: https://bit.ly/3gKVrGX.

3. On an Android test device (that meets the minimum requirements), go through the normal out-of-box setup steps, including adding a Google account (you will need

it to access the Play Store).

4. Search the Google Play Store for "Company Portal".

5. Once you've downloaded the Company Portal app, open it and sign in with the Intune licensed test user account.

6. After successfully signing in, you'll reach a screen with three setup steps: *Create work profile*, *Activate work profile* and *Update device settings*. Tap *Begin* to kick things off.

7. Follow the remaining setup steps and you'll end up with a device that is successfully enrolled and configured in work profile mode. You'll notice that some apps (like the Company Portal) now have a briefcase icon on them to denote that they are work apps.

8. Go back to the MEM admin center (https://endpoint.microsoft.com). Under *Devices > Android devices* you will see your newly enrolled device.

Android enrollment for corporate devices

With the three corporate Android management modes (Dedicated, Fully Managed and Fully Managed with work profile), you have a significantly improved selection of options for enrollment. You can choose from a some very slick, streamlined flows to get devices up and running. The flows are optimized for scenarios where devices are shipped directly to the place they will be used and set up with minimal or zero touch (as opposed the BYOD scenario, which assumes the user has already set up their device for personal use before adding the work stuff). These are some of the enrollment methods available to corporate-owned Android devices:

EMM Token is the process where you can skip out of the standard Android setup screens to instead perform Android Enterprise enrollment using a token (the token is a code that you type in). It's available in Android 6.0 and earlier, which means it is a good option for bootstrapping older Android devices into Android Enterprise. Once you go through a few secret steps and keypresses on the device, you'll end up at a screen where you can either scan the QR code or type the token manually.

QR Code is the same as token entry but more convenient. First, as with Token entry, you'll generate an enrollment token in MEM which you could then print on posters, send vie email or place somewhere on your intranet so that once the enrolling person gets a shipment of new devices, they'll only have to go through a few steps and key presses. The QR code method is available on Android 7.0 and up where you can tap the first setup screen six times to get started.

Near Field Communication (NFC) enrollment is one step better than QR code because it's contactless! Have you ever been to a conference and had your ID tag scanned with a NFC reader? You could magic something like this together for enrolling Android devices. The process for getting this up and running is a little more involved, though, since you'll need to buy some specialized NFC equipment (tags will cost about $22USD and a NFC programming app is free). One other benefit this method has over the others is that you can also encode your company's Wi-Fi connection details into the NFC to cut out one more step needed at enrollment time.

Zero Touch is the gold standard for enrolling corporate-owned devices. If you are familiar with Apple enrollment terminology, then it's the Android equivalent of the ADE program. When it's time to purchase new devices, your carrier or device reseller can offer Zero Touch as an option. The reseller can then ensure that all the devices you bought are populated into your company's own Zero Touch portal. In Google's Zero Touch portal, you will add your MEM enrollment token and then assign devices to it. Now, the reseller could send the devices directly to users or to work sites and all they would need is internet connectivity (either via SIM card or Wi-Fi) to automatically enroll into management.

Tip! – Google Zero Touch is set to support more manufacturers

At the time of writing this book, Google announced plans to support all Android 9.0+ devices, including those from other manufacturers, for the Zero Touch program. Read more about the announcement here: http://bit.ly/3a76BE3.

The table below summarizes the OS requirements for each enrollment type:

	Dedicated	Fully Managed	Fully Managed with work profile
EMM Token	Supported on Android 6.0+	Supported on Android 6.0+	Supported on Android 6.0+
QR Code	Supported on Android 7.0+	Supported on Android 7.0+	Supported on Android 7.0+
NFC	Supported on Android 6.0+	Supported on Android 6.0+	Supported on Android 6.0+
Zero Touch	Not Supported	Supported	Supported

Do it – Try out Android Enterprise corporate enrollment with a QR code

1. First you will set up an Android Enterprise enrollment profile for dedicated devices and construct a QR code. To do that, head to the MEM admin center (https://endpoint.microsoft.com) and then *Devices > Android > Android Enrollment*.

2. Select *Corporate-owned dedicated devices*, then *Create profile*.

3. Give the new profile a name like "Kiosk devices".

4. In the *Token type* drop-down, select *Corporate owned dedicated device (default)*.

5. Change or accept the default token expiry date (note that enrollment tokens are only valid for a maximum of 90 days, but you can easily replace them in the MEM admin center).

6. Once you've created the enrollment profile, you can select it, then under *Token* choose *Show token*.

7. Keep that token handy. Take a screenshot of it or print it off – you will use it to enroll devices.

Tip! – Azure AD shared mode

The token creation wizard gives you an option to choose the *Token type* in which you could choose *Azure AD shared mode*. If you use this type, the device gets the Azure AD Authenticator app installed. The reason for installing Authenticator is that the app can cause all corporate apps to be signed in our signed out with a single touch. Choose this option if your Android Enterprise Kiosk device has apps like Microsoft Teams or Outlook where users need to sign in to them. If your dedicated Android device is intended to only run a single app, or an app with no authentication, then the default option (without shared mode) is the right choice.

8. Power on a new or factory-reset Android device that meets the minimum requirements for Android Enterprise QR code enrollment.

9. Tap the first screen five times to enter the QR code scanner.

10. Scan the QR code that you generated. At this point you may be prompted to connect to a Wi-Fi network.

11. Follow the remaining device setup steps. At the end, the device will be enrolled into dedicated mode. You can tell when this completes as the *Intune* app will be installed on the device.

12. Now that you enrolled a dedicated device, work through the same steps for "Fully Managed" and "Fully Managed with work profile" enrollment tokens.

Getting started with Windows 10 enrollment

All up, I count eleven different flavors of enrollment for Windows 10 devices! Some of them for BYOD, some corporate and others could be used in either case. Your choice of enrollment method is important as it can really affect how the device is able to be managed later down the track. Those choices of enrollment type are also going to affect the capabilities available to use in MEM.

Tip! – Mastering Windows 10 enrollment types

The matrix of enrollment types and capabilities is too big to fit in this book, but you can take a look at this blog post I wrote on the topic - http://bit.ly/3gSeAH5. The blog post has a matrix that details enrollment types, requirements, and capabilities of each.

Windows 10 enrollment for personal devices

Microsoft provides three BYOD methods for enrolling Windows devices:

Add a Work or School Account

This enrollment method is most used in BYOD scenarios. I've seen schools use it as the fastest way to get the personal laptops of students enrolled in order to push down modern applications used in lessons. Once you set up a few things in Azure AD and MEM, users can be instructed to go to Windows settings where they find the option: "set up a work or school account".

Modern App Sign-in

More of an optimization to the Add Work or School Account, the back-end setup for IT admins is the same. The only difference is that the enrollment process is triggered whenever a user signs into a modern app (for example, the UWP version of Microsoft OneNote) instead of the Windows settings app.

MDM-only enrollment

Buried away in Windows settings, under Accounts, is an option to enroll in MDM only. This is one of the original enrollment methods and I really don't recommend it for MEM. It only creates device enrollment objects into MEM and does not register a device object into Azure AD. This has a huge impact on how the device can be used and managed. For example, because it is not registered in Azure AD it cannot participate in Conditional Access (We'll deep-dive on CA in Chapter 9).

Do it – Try out Windows 10 personal device enrollment

1. Go to the MEM admin center (https://endpoint.microsoft.com) and sign in.

2. On the left navigation menu, choose *Devices*, *Windows* and then *Windows enrollment*.

3. Select *Automatic enrollment*.

4. In the *MDM User scope* section, change the toggle from *None* to *All*. Leave the other settings at their default values.

Tip! – No need to change MDM user scopes

The MDM User scope page is an Azure AD Premium feature embedded into the MEM console for convenience. The Azure AD feature exists to provide a seamless setup and enrollment experience for Azure AD and BYOD devices across MEM and other MDM products. When using Intune, the discovery and enrollment URL's do not need to be changed at all – they are pre-configured.

By selecting *All* in the toggle, you are telling Azure AD that whenever it registers a Windows 10 device in Azure AD, it should automatically enroll that device into MDM. If you do not want to enable that for all users in your organization, you could scope that process down by choosing *Some* and then choosing a user group.

So, when does Azure AD register device into Azure AD? It happens when a user goes to settings and chooses "Add work or school account" or sets up the device from OOBE with their Azure AD user credentials. It can also be registered if a user signs into a modern Windows app such as OneNote or the Store.

If this automatic MDM enrollment for BYOD devices rings alarm bells for you, I recommend you use the Enrollment Restrictions feature we discussed earlier and block "Personal devices" from enrolling into MEM.

5. On a Windows 10 test device go to *Settings > Accounts > Access work or school*.

6. Select *Connect*.

Tip! – Local admin rights are needed!

A user must be a member of the local *Administrators* group on the device to enroll it into MEM. If they are not a local admin, the device registration into Azure AD can be successful but it will silently fail to enroll into management.

7. Sign in with the licensed Azure AD user account you created in an earlier exercise.

8. Follow the remaining wizard steps. At the end of the process, you will see your user's work account listed in settings. Click on it and you should see an *Info* button. (If you don't see that button, then chances are that the Azure AD device registration worked but MDM enrollment failed. You should go back and check your automatic enrollment and Intune licenses).

9. Click on *Info* to get more information about the MDM enrollment, including some of the policies and apps that were delivered and the last sync time. You can come back to this screen anytime to force a sync with MEM to get the latest policies and apps.

10. Head back to the MEM console and you will see this device is now enrolled and appears in the *All devices* list.

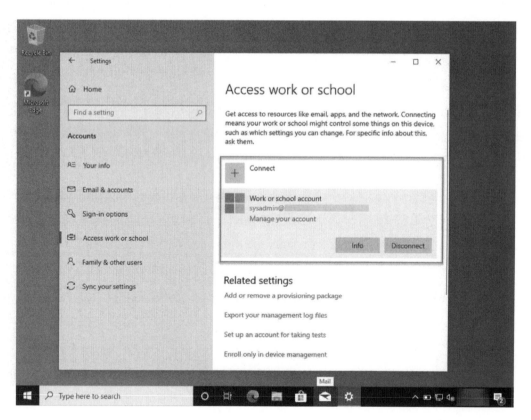

Windows 10 enrollment methods for (new) corporate devices

Microsoft Endpoint Manager supports many of the Windows 10 options for bootstrapping new corporate devices into management. Each method has its own pros and cons that need to be considered along with the device's usage scenario. In this section, I'm focusing on the most common and useful enrollment methods for new devices; by new devices, I mean you are unboxing them for the first time, they are not joined to any domain or under any management. I will cover bringing your existing (on-prem) device fleet into management in the co-management section. Here are the different methods for enrolling new devices into MEM:

Autopilot

Autopilot is a great automated enrollment process for corporate Windows devices. It is the Microsoft equivalent of Apple's ADE or Google's Zero Touch programs. The Autopilot value proposition is that devices can be pre-registered by device suppliers directly into Autopilot and shipped ready to users. When users power on an Autopilot registered device, it knows which organization it belongs to and will be joined to a directory (either Azure AD or on-prem Active Directory) and bootstrapped into MEM management where it will be configured with all the right settings, configuration and apps. There are four key flavors of Autopilot to meet different usage scenarios:

- **Autopilot (User-Driven with Azure AD Join)** is the original and most basic scenario. Users receive the device directly from a device manufacturer or re-seller and walk through the out-of-box experience (OOBE) setup screens themselves. You, as the IT admin, can customize that OOBE flow, skipping non-relevant screens such as the licensing page or specifying that at the end of the process the user performing device setup is deemed a standard user and not a local device administrator. In user-driven mode, devices are automatically registered into Azure AD and managed in MEM.

- **Autopilot (User-Driven with Hybrid Azure AD Join)** is very similar to the original Autopilot user-driven mode. However, this mode is useful if you need to keep devices in on-prem Active Directory rather than purely into Azure AD. For this mode to work, you will need to set up a few more things in MEM. First, you will need a connector between MEM and Active Directory so that during the device setup, MEM can deliver an Active Directory offline domain-join blob. This blob will complete an Active Directory Join if it is within line-of-sight to a domain controller. That means it's on the same internal network and getting all the right DNS pointers to know how to locate the domain controller. If your new devices need to be AD-joined from outside the corporate network (like at an employee's own home) you will need to deploy and configure a VPN profile with MEM as an additional step so that devices can connect to a domain controller before allowing a user to attempt Windows sign-in.

- **Autopilot (User-Driven with Pre-Provisioning)**, formerly known as "white-glove", is an optional optimization that you can make within an Autopilot profile. Microsoft developed this mode based on feedback that the first-time setup process is shifted to end-users and can take a long time to complete (download all the applications and apply all the settings). Imagine you are asked to arrange a new laptop for your boss, and she is too impatient to walk through the whole first-time setup process herself (click through OOBE and wait for the installation of apps and policies). With pre-provisioning you can get your hands on the laptop first and run through the setup before handing it over to her. Once you enable pre-provisioning for an autopilot device, you can use a secret key sequence to escape normal OOBE and perform setup and enrollment on your boss's behalf. You can do the waiting for apps and policies to be installed before boxing it back up and handing it over. Your boss will have a super-quick, seamless experience the first time she opens the lid… and you will probably get a nice raise for it.

- **Autopilot (Self-Deploying mode)** is the most zero-touch flavor out of all Autopilot enrollment methods. This mode is designed to be used in kiosk-style scenarios. Think of digital signs or point-of-sale systems. The key difference for self-deploying mode is there is no user affinity. No user credentials are needed during the setup process. One important gotcha for this Autopilot mode is that there are some significant device hardware requirements; specifically, the requirement for a Trusted Platform Model (TPM) 2.0 chip. The reason for that is security – since there is no user password authentication needed during setup, the TPM provides the Autopilot service with strong attestation of its identity.

Azure AD Join (from OOBE)

For all corporate flavors of Windows 10 (all editions except Windows 10 home) there is a step in the OOBE setup flow where a user can choose if this device is being used for work or school. If the user chooses *work or school*, then they are headed down the user-driven Azure AD Join path without the guardrails of Autopilot. This enrollment method is fine, It's just not as personalized as the Autopilot flows. If the enrolling user is in the *MDM User Scope* and they are licensed, the device will be enrolled and ready for management with MEM.

Bulk enrollment with an Azure AD token

Bulk enrollment can be used as a fast way to set up corporate windows devices that are not registered in Autopilot. You can configure an Azure AD bulk enrollment token to be used inside a Windows 10 provisioning package and then applied to any or many PC's during the initial OOBE setup process. Doing this skips a whole bunch of setup steps. Another great advantage is that you can pre-configure Wi-Fi connection details in the package. Bulk enrollment does have one major drawback though – it's pretty high-touch. You need to load the provisioning package (a .PPKG file) onto a USB stick and physically plug that

USB stick into each PC that needs enrolling. This may be a lot more work than what you want to sign up for. I often see this form of enrollment used by IT admins at schools – the program for creating the package is called "Set up school PC" and is simple to use. The act of physically plugging in USB drives is usually offloaded to tech-savvy teachers at the schools where the devices need to be used.

> **Tip! – Install the Configuration Manager agent on new devices**
>
> New devices that are provisioned with any of the above modern provisioning techniques can easily have the Configuration Manager agent installed on them once they become enrolled into MEM. Deploying this agent to them effectively makes them "co-managed" which significantly increases the management capabilities available – for example, you will have the ability to deliver apps to them from the huge portfolio built up in Configuration Manager over the years. Read more about co-management in Chapter 12.

Do it – Try out Windows 10 enrollment: User-driven Azure AD Join

1. Go to the MEM admin center (https://endpoint.microsoft.com) and sign in.

2. On the left navigation menu choose *Devices > Windows* and then *Windows enrollment*.

3. Select *Automatic enrollment*.

4. In the *MDM User scope* section, change the toggle from *None* to *All*. Leave the other settings at their default values.

5. Now find a brand-new Windows 10 device. It should have a business version of Windows 10 installed. You may need to reset an existing one to get it back to the OOBE setup (I recommend using a VM running on Hyper-V for this exercise).

6. Power it on and walk through the blue OOBE screens (language, keyboard layout) until you get to the work account sign-in screen. The actual experience and screens will differ slightly depending on the version and edition of Windows 10 you use.

Tip! – Use virtual machine snapshots

For these enrollment exercises I highly recommend using VM's and taking snapshots. This will save you a ton of time in preparing devices ready for each enrollment type. My advice is to create a Windows 10 VM, install Windows 10 Professional on it, then snapshot it at the very first OOBE screen. This way you can roll back to the same snapshot for each exercise.

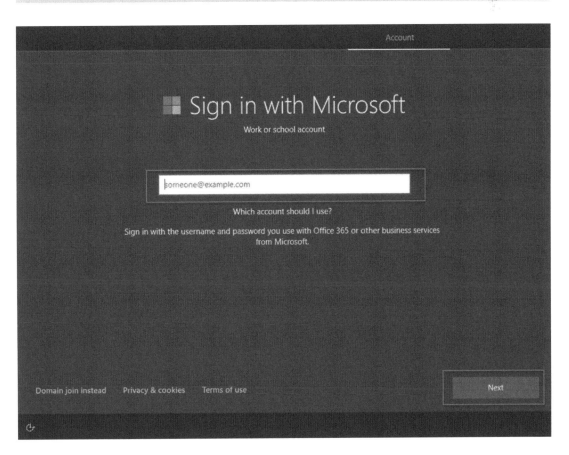

7. Sign in with one of your licensed test user account credentials.

8. The device will be set up, enrolled and logged into Windows.

9. Head back to the MEM admin center and check for a device in the *All devices* list.

Do it – Try out Windows 10 enrollment: Autopilot user-driven mode

In this exercise you will deploy a Windows 10 device with AutoPilot User-driven mode. First, you will need to gather the hardware hash of a Windows 10 device (either virtual or physical) into a .CSV file using PowerShell and then create and assign an Autopilot profile to it. You will then walk through enrolling that device using Autopilot.

- Part 1 – Harvest an Autopilot device hash.
- Part 2 – Create and assign an Autopilot profile.
- Part 3 – Enroll a device.

Part 1 – Harvest the Autopilot device hash.

1. Start with a brand-new VM or test device. It should have Windows 10 Professional or Enterprise already installed on it and be waiting at the blue OOBE screen.

2. Hold Shift + F10 on the keyboard. This will bring up a command prompt.

3. Type *PowerShell* into the command prompt and then hit enter to convert to a Microsoft PowerShell window.

4. Type the following commands, followed by enter:

```
Install-Script -Name Get-WindowsAutoPilotInfo
Y
Set-ExecutionPolicy bypass
Get-WindowsautoPilotInfo.Ps1 -Online
```

5. You will be prompted for a username and password. Type the credentials for the MEM admin account.

6. Watch the script complete. First, it will connect to your tenant and then gather and import the hash. You should eventually see a message that says *All devices synced.*

Tip! – Autopilot hash harvesting!

In real-life it is unlikely that you would need to manually harvest Autopilot device ID's via a PowerShell script. Instead, your organization starts an Autopilot arrangement with a preferred device re-seller where they act on your behalf to automatically register devices into your environment whenever you create a new device order. The registration process for OEM's and CSP's is documented here: http://bit.ly/36H1Pv2.

The manual PowerShell method is just a way for you to test out Autopilot before you move on to the real thing – It's similar to the dance we did in the Apple Enrollment section to manually register devices into ADE using Apple Configurator.

If you have thousands of devices in MEM that didn't enroll via Autopilot, but you want to ensure they do if they are ever reset, you can harvest in bulk by deploying a special type of Autopilot profile. When creating the profile, you can enable the option – *Convert all targeted devices to Autopilot.*

Convert all targeted devices to Autopilot ⓘ	No	Yes

Part 2 – Create and assign an Autopilot profile.

7. On your admin PC, go to the MEM admin center (https://endpoint.microsoft.com) and sign in.

8. On the left navigation menu choose *Devices > Windows* and then *Windows enrollment.*

9. Select *Devices – Manage Windows Autopilot devices.*

10. In the list of devices, you should see the one you just uploaded.

11. Click on the device and, in the context pane that opens, notice how you can rename

it and assign a group tag even before the device is set up and enrolled into MEM. You could use either of these properties (device name or group tag) to create an Azure AD dynamic device group.

12. Notice on the *Devices* page that there are alternative ways to add devices to Auto-pilot such as the *Import* capability.

13. Use the *Enroll devices* breadcrumb to get back to the *Windows enrollment* menu, then select *Deployment profiles*.

14. Select *Create profile > Windows PC*.

15. Add a name and description for the profile and leave the other options on the *Basics* page default.

16. On the *Out-of-box experience (OOBE)* page, accept the default deployment mode of *User-driven* and Azure AD Join type as *Azure AD joined*.

17. Review and configure any of the OOBE customization settings and then move to the *Assignments* page.

18. On the *Assignments* page, select *All devices* from the dropdown. You could optionally create a dynamic or static device group before getting to this step to limit the scope, but since this environment has only one device it will not hurt to deploy to a large scope.

19. Review and save the configuration.

20. Before moving onto the next step, select the profile you just created and then select the *Assigned devices* option. Make sure you can see your autopilot device in this list (warning – this could take up to an hour).

Part 3 – Enroll a device.

21. Head back to the test device or VM where you grabbed the Autopilot device ID and restart it. You could type Restart-computer from the open PowerShell window.

22. As the device restarts it will have a customized OOBE experience based on the Autopilot profile you created and assigned. You will eventually see a "Welcome to *tenant name*" user sign-in screen.

Tip! – OOBE Branding

The branding you see in this Out-Of-Box-Experience (OOBE) screen is based on what you have configured in Azure AD. You can easily customize this to make it familiar for your end-users. To upload your own branding images, go to https://portal.azure.com > Azure Active Directory > Company Branding and then upload your own branding images.

To save you from messing around with image dimensions and file sizes I have created a branding pack for you that you can edit as you like and then upload. https://bit.ly/3rMhGAr.

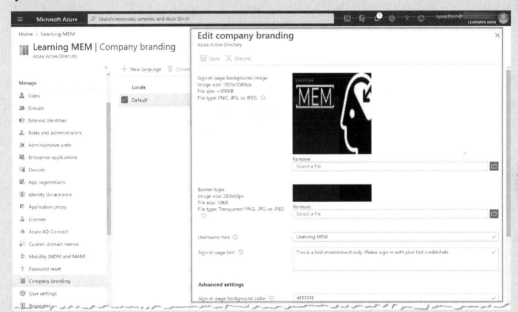

For more information on Azure AD branding, take a look at Microsoft's online docs: http://bit.ly/34yrQvf.

23. Sign in with your test user credentials and wait for the rest of the setup steps to complete. Depending on your MEM configuration, the user might be prompted for

additional information such as a Windows Hello for Business Setup – Windows Hello is enabled by default but you can disable it in MEM by going to *Windows enrollment, Windows Hello for Business*.

24. After the user is logged in, head back to the MEM admin center and verify that a new device ID has been created under *Devices > All devices*.

Tip! – Make users wait for setup to finish

If you want users to wait for setup to finish completely before they land on a desktop, then you can optionally deploy an Enrollment Status Page (ESP) profile in MEM. You have many options for this profile, including choosing which apps to wait for, how long to wait and what error messages to show users if the process fails.

Explore the settings further by going to *Windows enrollment, Enrollment Status Page*. Step-by-step instructions for creating ESP profiles are included in the Microsoft documentation http://bit.ly/3aYTYdd.

Try out more Autopilot scenarios!

Now that you've deployed an Autopilot profile to a device, I recommend trying out some of the other Autopilot configurations by following Microsoft docs:

Try out the Pre-provisioned (previously known as "White-glove") profile type. (http://bit.ly/38w48RQ).

Try out the "Hybrid Azure AD Join" option (http://bit.ly/3nJ14I8).

Try out Self-deploying mode: http://bit.ly/3h9vzVe.

Do it – Try out Windows 10 enrollment with a bulk enrollment token

In this exercise you will use the Windows Configuration Designer tool to create an Azure AD bulk enrollment token, then you will apply it to a fresh Windows 10 device.

- Part 1 – Create a bulk enrolment token.
- Part 2 – Enroll a device using a bulk enrollment token.

Part 1 – Create a bulk enrollment token.

1. On your administration machine, go to the Microsoft Store app and search for "Windows Configuration Designer". If you can't find it in a search, try this short URL: http://bit.ly/3azbXJ4.
2. Install the app, then launch it from the start menu.
3. On the start page, under *Create*, select *Provision desktop devices*. Then type a name and description.

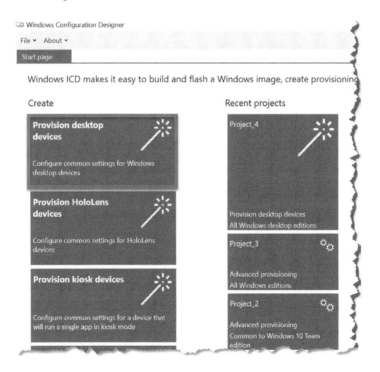

4. Browse through the available options for the configuration package. Under *Device name*, type a naming convention for the provisioned devices. This device name can be used later for grouping and identifying devices in the MEM admin center.

5. On the *Set up network* step, type the Network SSID and connection details for the Wi-Fi network for the location where devices will be set up. If you plan to plug in a wired connection, then you can ignore this step.

6. On the *Account management* step, select *Enroll in Azure AD*, then *Get bulk token*.

7. Provide the username and password of your MEM admin account. This credential is required to generate the token that will later be used to enroll devices.

8. Configure any of the other optional settings, then select *Create*. Take note of the output path where you can find the created provisioning package (.ppkg file).

9. Copy the provisioning package to the root of a removable USB drive.

Tip! – There is no USB drive option in Hyper-V

If you plan to use a Microsoft Hyper-V VM as the test device I recommend copying the provisioning package to a virtual DVD drive – this is because they are nice and easy to attach to Hyper-V VM's during OOBE.

I download and use a free tool called *Folder2Iso* to first create an ISO file that will represent a virtual DVD 'disk' and then I double-click it to attach it to Windows as a virtual disk. After the virtual disk is attached to my Windows 10 management PC, I copy the provisioning package to it. Lastly, I disconnect the drive from Windows using the right-click option from explorer and then attach it to my VM as a DVD drive.

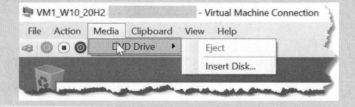

LEARNING MICROSOFT ENDPOINT MANAGER

Part 2 – Enroll a device with a bulk enrollment token.

10. Find or prepare a fresh Windows 10 device and have it ready at the first OOBE screen. Make sure you've set up network connectivity for it (either you have added Wi-Fi details in the PPKG or you have directly attached a wired network connection).

11. Insert the provisioning package. For physical devices, insert the USB drive and for VM's, attach the DVD drive. Windows will automatically read and recognize the provisioning package from a removable USB drive and begin applying the package. For DVD drives, you will need to hit the Windows key on the keyboard five times in a row to get to a menu. Select *Install provisioning package* to kick things off.

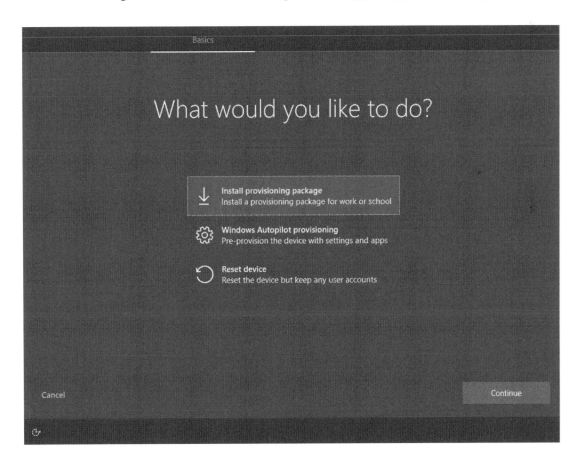

12. The device will now move through the steps of joining Azure AD and enrolling in MEM.

13. At the end of the enrollment process, log into the device with an Azure AD test user account.

14. Head back to the MEM admin center and verify that the device has been enrolled into management successfully. You should see a device object under the *Devices > All devices* page.

Tip! – Try out Set up a School PC App

In this exercise we used *Windows configuration designer* but there is another app that Microsoft develops specifically for school scenarios. The app has the advantage of being a lot more user-friendly – it is developed with School teachers or IT generalists in mind. Try it out by searching the Windows app store or go to this link directly (http://bit.ly/34Qne47) to download it.

Windows 10 enrollment for existing corporate devices

The following enrollment methods can be used to bring existing on-prem Domain Joined Windows 10 PC's into management with MEM. If you are using Configuration Manager for PC management in your organization, then I recommend focusing on the co-management method which we cover in more depth in Chapter 12. If you do not have Configuration Manager at your workplace, that's not a problem – you can use the Automatic MDM Enrollment Group Policy method.

Co-management enrollment

Configuration Manager is by far the most popular method for managing Windows PC's in small, medium and enterprise environments. The good news is that you can connect all those devices already under ConfigMan management to Intune and make them "co-managed" – that means they are managed by both Intune and Configuration Manager simultaneously. Once they are in this "co-managed" state you deliver workloads (such as apps and or policies) from either Configuration Manager management points or Intune in the cloud and manage the device in either console. Microsoft has worked hard to make this enrollment method as simple as possible but there are some prerequisites. The key steps involve setting up Azure AD device registration, enabling co-management via a wizard and then choosing which workloads (e.g., Apps, profile types) you want to manage in Intune and which ones you'd rather stay in ConfigMan. We will take a closer look at co-management in Chapter 12, including enrollment walkthroughs.

Automatic MDM Enrollment Group Policy

Environments without Configuration Manager can deploy a Group Policy setting to trigger enrollment into MEM. Under the hood, this method is similar to co-management in that first a Hybrid Azure AD Join is performed, followed by the MDM enrollment. Once you enable the Group Policy setting, a scheduled task will fire every time a user signs into Windows 10 and the device will attempt an Azure AD Device Join. Every 15 minutes a second scheduled task will then attempt to enroll the device into MEM in the background.

Tip! – Automatic MDM Enrollment requires Hybrid Azure AD Join

An important pre-requisite for automatically enrolling any existing on-prem Domain-Joined devices into MEM is enabling Azure AD device registration. This step is crucial for both co-management enrollment and Automatic MDM enrollment via group policy. We will cover the steps to enable Hybrid Azure AD Join in Chapter 12.

Tip! – Group Policy setting name

The Group Policy setting name and options have been updated a few times at each Windows 10 release as more features were added to the operating system. If you see a difference in the setting name and configurable options in the environment where you are working, you are probably just using an older version of Windows 10 with older Administrative Template definitions and you can resolve that by working on a management PC that has the latest Windows 10 release.

Advanced enrollment concepts – DEM, enrollment restrictions and customization

Now that you have mastered the different types of enrollment, let's take a look at some more advanced enrollment features of MEM.

Device Enrollment Manager (DEM)

The Device Enrollment Manager (DEM) account is a super-special account used for enrolling userless devices. Think of it as a service account. It's not a real user but an Azure AD user account that can be used to provision devices that don't need any user affinity. A single DEM account can be used to enroll 1000 devices (instead of the usual 15 devices per user limit). Before you start getting ideas about saving licensing costs you should look at the limitations – there are lots. My advice is to use this account only as a last resort in provisioning scenarios – for example, if you need to set up a kiosk-based Windows device and you cannot use Autopilot Zero Touch because the device does not meet the hardware requirements. To use a DEM account, you must first create a new Azure AD user account and assign it with an Intune license. It can then be promoted to a DEM account under *Devices > Enroll Devices > Device enrollment managers*.

Enrollment restrictions

Enrollment restrictions lay out the rules for enrolling devices. These rules are split across two slightly different categories in the MEM admin center – Device Types and Device Limits. Both restrictions come with a configurable default policy that applies to the entire organization, or you can create more specific user-targeted restrictions.

Enrollment restrictions – Device types

Device Type restriction policies allow you to specify which platforms are allowed to enroll into MEM and start receiving the policies, apps and certificates. Not only can you choose to allow or block specific platforms, but you can also dive into more granular restrictions based on OS versions, manufacturers or ownership (personal versus corporate devices).

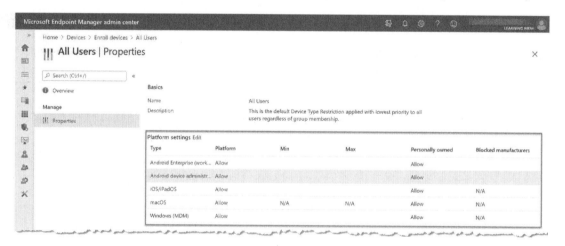

Tip! – Personal versus corporate devices

How does MEM know if devices are personally owned? While MEM cannot know who physically paid for a device, it can infer device ownership by looking at the enrollment method used. For example, any device that was enrolled via the Apple Automated Device Enrollment (ADE) program clearly belongs to the organization. The other way is to use a feature called "Corporate device identifiers", in which you can define a list of corporate devices manually. You can see whether a device is marked corporate or personal under *Devices > All Devices > Select device > Overview*. You can also change the ownership property manually under the device's *Properties* page.

Enrollment restrictions – Device limits

Device limit policies are used to customize the number of devices users can enroll in MEM. The default value is five and the maximum configurable is 15 devices. Although you might scoff at each user needing to enroll 15 devices into management, I find it generally helpful to configure this value on the higher side to account for device turn-over. For example, if Betty from HR gets a new laptop, company phone, personal desk phone and tablet to replace her old ones, the limit of five devices would not be enough for her. She'd want to enroll the new devices before her existing ones are aged out of service.

Tip! – Azure AD has its own device limits outside of MEM

Device enrollment is a two-part process – Part 1 is the Azure AD registration and Part 2 is a MEM enrollment. The device limit restrictions we've discussed so far only control Part 2. When you increase the enrollment limits in MEM it's important that you also go to the Azure AD and increase that limit, too. The Azure AD limit is a global, organization-wide setting that can be changed under *Portal.azure.com > Azure Active Directory > Devices > Device settings* and then *Maximum number of devices per user*. Most customers I've worked with over the years set the Azure AD limit to 'Unlimited' to prevent helpdesk calls down the track.

Tip! – Some enrollment types do not have a device limit!

Some enrollment methods are considered "non-user affinity". This is another way of saying the enrollment happened without any clue of which user was involved. During the enrollment, no users had to enter a username and password and instead were driven by IT people using token-based authentication for the device. These methods of enrollment will ignore device limits:

Co-management, Automatic MDM Enrollment Group Policy, Azure AD join, Bulk enrollment, Autopilot, DEM

Enrollment Status Page (ESP) for Windows 10 devices

The enrollment status page is a feature introduced in Windows 10 version 1803. The page is shown to end-users during the OOBE setup flow and other users the first time they sign in to a Windows 10 device. The purpose of the ESP is to stall users from continuing to the desktop while giving them a nice progress page until all the right policies and applications are applied in the background. It works no matter what type of enrollment was used – both for Autopilot enrollments and user-driven Azure AD join.

You can configure and customize the enrollment status page in the *Devices > Enroll devices > Windows enrollment* page of the MEM admin center.

Tip! – A device can only have one ESP profile on it…ever!

Once you deploy an ESP configuration to a device it stays there for the entire life of the device. That means that if multiple users are signing on, they will all receive the same configuration on that device even if they are targeted with different policies.

To see the full list of settings, refer to the Microsoft documentation here: https://bit.ly/3aYTYdd.

Automatic enrollment for Windows 10 devices

On new tenants, there is an important step admins need to take before starting to enroll Windows 10 devices. Azure AD provides a feature called Automatic enrollment with their Azure AD premium license, which triggers an automatic MDM enrollment upon registering devices into Azure AD.

On the *Automatic enrollment* page, you need to toggle the "MDM user scope" to a value of "Some" while you are testing things out or "All" when you're in the full swing of device management. Don't touch the other options on this page – the discovery URL's only exist because this screen is used for configuring other UEM products which may need these options configured.

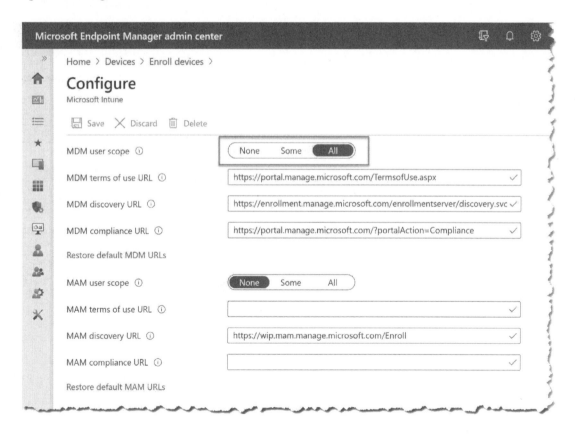

> **Tip! – MAM user scope**
>
> Stay away from the MAM user scope for now too. This is used only for Windows 10 app protection (also known as Windows Information Protection), which we will cover in Chapter 7.

Corporate device identifiers

Corporate device identifiers, for iOS and Android devices, allow you to manually pre-configure a list of "Corporate" devices. You create a list of devices by specifying their unique serial numbers and MEM will check this list each time a device enrolls. If the device is on the list it will be stamped with a "Corporate" tag. Device identifiers are most useful when enrolling iOS/iPadOS and macOS devices that are corporate-owned but were not purchased through a corporate program such as ADE. Read more about the device identifiers here: https://bit.ly/2QuNSYy.

> **Tip! – Use corporate device identifiers during MDM migration projects**
>
> If you are migrating devices from a different Endpoint Management product to MEM and are not planning on factory-resetting them, you should consider exporting all the serial numbers from the old product and then importing them to MEM. This way they will automatically be marked corporate no matter which method you use to enroll them.

Company Portal customization and branding

When it comes to user-driven enrollments, you can improve the enrollment experience that users have within the Company Portal app. Settings are tweakable by creating and assigning customization policies under *Tenant administration > Customization*. Customization settings can be defined in a default policy or you can choose to create customization profiles and assign them to different groups of users. There are three buckets of settings that admins customize:

- **Branding** – Choose the overall branding settings for users when they sign in to the Company Portal app or website on any device. You can define the colors, logos and organization names.

- **Support information** – Define the support contact information that users see in the Company Portal app. Define contact name, phone number, email address, website name and URL, or free text for additional support details (for example, the support operating hours).

- **Configuration** – Customize the functionality of the Company Portal app for users. You can choose to hide enrollment prompts for users if you'd prefer them to use MAM instead of MDM. Alternatively, you can customize privacy messages and preferences for push notifications. The Company Portal experiences can be further customized for apps – letting you bring in apps that were targeted outside of MEM – such as Azure AD and Office. There are also options to hide self-service functionality from end-users; for example, you can hide remote device reset from users in the app.

Do it – Try out customization and branding

1. Sign in to the MEM admin center and then go to *Tenant Administration > Customization*.

2. Edit the default policy and tweak the branding, support information and configuration settings.

Tip! – Download sample branding images

To save you from messing around with images and getting dimensions and file size, you can download, edit and apply images from a sample pack I created for this book. Download it here: https://bit.ly/3jMU2B1.

3. Now open the Company Portal app on each test device to see the resulting end-user experience. If you do not have any test devices handy at this point you can use the web experience to experiment – just go to the URL https://portal.manage.micro-soft.com and sign in with a licensed test user account.

CHAPTER 4

REMOTE DEVICE ACTIONS

When most people think of "management" their first consideration is device actions – remotely triggering things like a device lock, reset or device sync. This chapter covers both the actions that are available to you as a MEM administrator but also the actions that a user can perform in a self-service manner from the Company Portal. We will explore some of the platform differences and requirements related to device actions, too.

Admin device actions

The remote actions available from the MEM admin center vary based on a few factors, including platform limitations as well as privacy and ownership considerations. For example, there are more wipe options available for Windows 10 PC's than other platforms and MEM restricts actions that IT admins can take on personal devices.

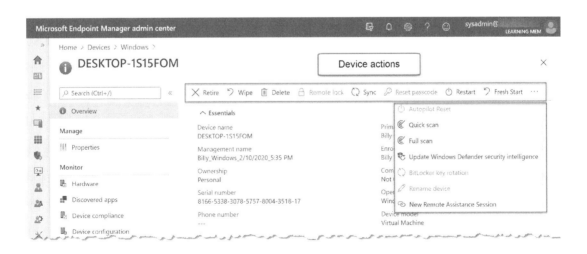

Common device actions

The following device actions are available in MEM:

- **Retire** – Use the Retire remote action to remove the device from management but not factory reset it. Under the hood, the device will check-in and remove all management certificates. Although the device is no longer managed, the device object will stay in the MEM admin center until you manually clean it up or it is aged out using automatic cleanup rules.

- **Wipe** – Sends a factory reset message to the device. Once a device is wiped it must be manually re-enrolled into MEM. For Windows 10, there is a special option, "Retain enrollment state and user account", where you can choose to keep the device enrolled and keep the user profile data after it is wiped.

- **Delete** – Does everything that the "Retire" action does plus cleans up the device object from the admin center device list.

- **Remote lock** – Sends a push notification to the device along with a lock command. When a device has been remotely locked, the user must unlock it with their passcode. For a remote lock to work, the device must have already had a PIN set.

- **Sync** – Tells the device to wake up and check in with MEM to get policy.

- **Reset passcode** – Resets the device-level passcode. For Android, only the work profile passcode is reset, and the experience is such that a temporary passcode is created. This action is not supported for iOS; instead, there is a specific action – "remove passcode".

- **Restart** – Shuts down the device and powers it back on. The end-user experience varies by platform but generally, users won't be notified before the device reboots.

- **New Remote Assistance Session** – Requires integration with a third-party remote assistance product called TeamViewer. You must first configure the integration in

Tenant admin > Connectors and tokens > TeamViewer connector and devices must also have the TeamViewer app installed on them. TeamViewer is not included in MEM licensing; it must be purchased separately.

- **Rename device** – Allows you to remotely set a new name on the device. The new name will be set both in the device settings and in the MEM portal. If you would like to simply update the device name in the portal without initiating a device action, you can update the device's "Management name" under *Devices > all devices > [device] > Properties > Management name*.

- **Send custom notification** – On mobile devices you can craft a short message including a title (50 characters maximum) and body (500 characters maximum) to be delivered to mobile devices as a push notification. The Company Portal mobile app must be installed on the remote device to receive the notification.

iOS/iPadOS device actions

The below actions are specific to the iOS/iPadOS platform:

- **Remove passcode** – This action is like "Reset passcode", however the action removes the existing user passcode and prompts the user to create a new one in settings.

- **Shutdown** – Sends a remote shutdown command to supervised iOS/iPadOS devices.

- **Lost mode** – Supervised iOS/iPadOS devices can be remotely placed into "Lost mode" by IT admins. When a device is placed into lost mode, you also provide a message and contact phone number which will display on the lock screen for whoever picks up the device. Hopefully, they phone you to return it. If you do not get that phone call you could try some other actions such as "Play lost mode sound" or "Locate device". When in "Lost mode" the device is blocked from use until you disable it in the MEM admin center.

- **Locate device** – Shows the GPS co-ordinates on a map of the last device (supervised iOS/iPadOS only) known location. To use this action you must first use the "Lost mode" action.

- **Play lost mode sound** – Sends a command to the device to play the "ding-dinga-ding-ding" sound repeatedly until the device is removed from lost mode or the user disables sound. To use this action the device needs to be supervised and first placed into "Lost mode".

- **Log out current user** – When iOS/iPadOS devices are operating in Apple "Shared mode" they can have many users log in and out of them using managed Apple ID's from the lock screen. This remote action can be used to log the current user out so that others may log in.

macOS device actions

The following device actions are specific for macOS devices:

- **Rotate FileVault recovery key** – If a user's FileVault recovery key is spent (the user themselves or an IT admin retrieved it to recover an encrypted device) then it is a good idea to rotate that key. Admins can trigger this process manually as a remote action for macOS devices.

- **Erase** – Action is available for macOS devices and removes the entire operating system. At the time of issuing the action you must add a recovery pin. The recovery pin can be handed to a user in order to re-install the OS.

Windows 10 device actions

The below remote device actions are specific to the Windows 10 platform:

- **Fresh start** – Windows 10 "Fresh start" is a feature that is supposed to remove any OEM bloatware (pre-installed apps) on new PC's. You can trigger this remotely for any enrolled Windows 10 device and decide at the same time whether to retain user profile data. This action will remove the device from MEM management temporarily but since it remains Azure AD joined it will enroll again when the first user signs in.

- **Autopilot reset** – Removes all profile data, apps and settings but keeps the device enrolled in MEM. This reset type is often useful in schools where devices are reset at the end of the school term and are ready to be handed on to the next set of students. One key difference between Autopilot reset and "Wipe" is that the former does not give you a choice to keep some user data on the device.

- **Quick scan** – Triggers Windows 10 devices to start a quick antivirus scan using Microsoft Defender. A quick scan looks at locations such as registry keys and startup folders.

- **Full scan** – Triggers Windows 10 devices to perform a full scan, which takes a deeper look, checking all files and running programs on a hard disk.

- **Update Windows Defender security intelligence** – Remotely triggers Windows 10 devices to update their Microsoft Defender signatures.

- **BitLocker key rotation** – For any Azure AD joined or Hybrid Azure AD joined devices, BitLocker encryption keys are synced into Azure AD where they can be retrieved by users (via self-service) or by an IT admin in the MEM admin center. If a key is spent (used by either party to recover a locked-out device) then it is a good idea to trigger key rotation manually with this action.

Remote Action	iOS	macOS	Windows 10	Android Enterprise
Common device actions				
Retire	Supported	Supported	Supported	Supported (WP only)
Wipe	Supported (Device enrollment only)	Not supported	Supported	Supported
Delete	Supported	Supported	Supported	Supported
Remote lock	Supported	Supported	Not supported	Supported (all)
Sync	Supported	Supported	Supported	Supported (WP only)
Reset passcode	Not Supported (Use remove passcode instead)	Not Supported	Not Supported	Supported. (Check OS requirements)
Restart	Supported (supervised only)	Not supported	Supported	Supported (WP only)
New Remote Assistance Session	Supported	Supported	Supported	Supported (WP only)
Rename device	Supported (Supervised only)	Not supported	Supported (AADJ only)	Not supported
Send custom notification	Supported	Not Supported	Not Supported	Supported (WP only)
iOS/iPadOS only actions				
Remove passcode	Supported (device enrollment only)			
Shutdown	Supported (Supervised only)			
Lost mode	Supported (Supervised only)			
Locate device	Supported (Supervised only)			
Play lost mode sound	Supported (Supervised only)			
Logout current user	Supported (Supervised + Shared iPad only)			

macOS only actions			
Erase		Supported	
Rotate FileVault recovery key		Supported (OS 10.13 and later)	
Windows 10 only actions			
Fresh start			Supported	
Autopilot reset			Supported	
Quick scan			Supported	
Full scan			Supported	
Update Windows Defender security intelligence			Supported	
BitLocker key rotation			Supported (AADJ or HAADJ only)	

Do it – Try out device actions

In this exercise you will get familiar with device actions available on different platforms. I recommend trying out a few to get familiar with the admin and end-user experiences.

1. Go to the MEM admin center and sign in.

2. Go to *Devices > All devices* and select any enrolled device.

3. View the list of actions on the *Overview* page.

4. Try out triggering different device actions. I recommend starting with the least-destructive actions first – for example, sync, restart, scan and rename – before getting into actions such as device wipe.

Bulk device actions

Building upon the ability to perform remote actions on a single device, you might find it useful to trigger actions for many devices at the same time. The MEM admin center allows you to perform bulk device actions but has a maximum selection limit of 100 devices. You can perform bulk actions from the *All devices* page under the *Bulk device actions* navigation item.

The following actions are supported in bulk:

- Autopilot reset

- Custom notifications

- Delete

- Rename

- Restart

- Sync

- Wipe

- Retire

Do it – Try out bulk device actions

In this exercise you'll get familiar with the bulk device actions feature.

1. Go to the MEM admin center and sign in.

2. Go to *Devices > All devices*.

3. Select *Bulk device actions* at the top of the page.

4. On the *Bulk device actions* page, select an OS (for which you have more than one device enrolled) and then choose an action (for example, sync).

5. On the *Devices* page, select a few devices then complete the wizard.

6. The remote action will be triggered on each of the devices.

End-user initiated device actions

Some device actions can be triggered by users when they are using the Company Portal app or website. This can help enable user self-service and reduce the burden on your support desk. For example, if a user realizes they left their work iPad in an Uber, they could just reach into their pocket and use the Company Portal app on their phone to remotely lock it until they find it again. User-driven device actions are labeled a bit differently from the IT admin ones in the MEM admin center, so I'll define them below.

The following actions are supported for user self-service:

*   **Remove** – This is the same as an IT admin "Retire" action. It removes the device from MEM.

- **Reset (or Factory reset)** – This action is the same as a "Wipe" command for IT admins. On the iOS Company Portal this action is called *Factory reset*.

- **Rename** – This action only changes the friendly device name that the user sees in the Company Portal and makes it easier for them to recognize their own devices. It does not issue an MDM command to rename.

- **Check access** – This action initiates a device check-in (Sync) with MEM.

- **Remote lock** – Works the same as the MEM admin center remote lock. The device's unlock PIN must be entered to unlock the device.

- **Reset passcode** – This action is used to reset the device passcode remotely from the Company Portal app or website.

- **Get recovery key** – Users may self-recover their FileVault key for managed macOS devices or their BitLocker key for Windows 10 right from the Company Portal website. This saves them from calling the helpdesk to retrieve it.

Action	iOS/iPadOS	macOS	Windows 10	Android Enterprise
Remove (Retire)	Supported (except ADE enrolled devices)	Supported	Supported (except on AADJ devices)	Supported (WP only)
Reset (Wipe)	Supported (except ADE enrolled devices)	Not supported	Supported	Supported (WP only)
Rename	Supported	Supported	Supported	Supported (WP only)
Check access (Sync)	Supported	Supported	Supported	Supported
Remote lock	Supported	Not Supported	Not Supported	Supported
Reset passcode	Supported	Not Supported	Not Supported	Supported (WP only)
Key recovery	Not Supported	Supported	Supported	Not Supported

Tip! – In a few cases, you can customize which actions you want to make available for users in the Company Portal

For example, you can define that you do not want to allow users to reset their corporate-owned Windows 10 devices because getting them enrolled again would be a real nightmare for your helpdesk. See Chapter 3 for more details on deploying MEM customization policies.

Do it – Try out self-service device actions

In this exercise you will get familiar with the end-user experiences for device actions. You will use the web portal to discover these actions. I recommend trying out these actions in the Company Portal app too.

1. Open a new InPrivate browser tab and go to the Company Portal website (www. manage.micrsooft.com). Sign in with a test-user account.

2. Use the left-nav menu to go to *Devices* then select a device.

3. Notice there are device actions available such as Check status, Rename and reset passcode. The actual options will vary based on the device you chose.

4. Try each of the actions across the different devices enrolled by your test user.

CHAPTER 5

CONFIGURING DEVICE SETTINGS

To control the look and feel of devices, MEM requires you to apply one or more configuration 'Profiles''. Profiles are groupings of similar settings – for example, a Wi-Fi profile contains all settings needed to control access to Wi-Fi, and Device restrictions is a bucket of lock-down settings for the platform. It's not possible for you to create just one big profile that contains all the possible configuration settings. For every profile you create, you will walk through the same steps – define a name, choose the settings, choose the group of users or devices to assign the profile to and, finally, review and create. In the next section I'll provide a high-level view of each of the profile types and common examples.

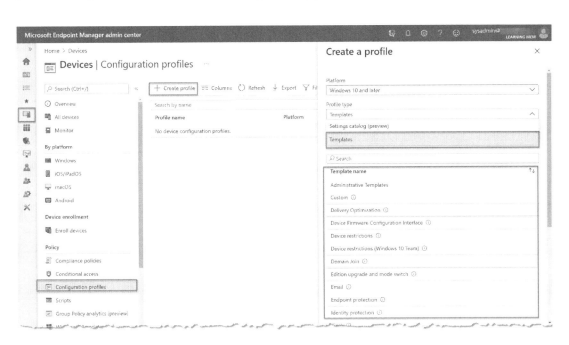

Tip! – New settings catalog (preview feature)

The MEM settings catalog is a new way of defining and deploying profiles. Instead of a fixed set of predefined profile types, IT admins can build their own "Profiles" using whatever settings they want. A "Profile" becomes an assignable unit, and you can add to it any setting you wish from a catalog. At the time of writing this book the settings catalog supports just Windows 10 and Edge settings on macOS but keep an eye out for this feature to expand further into the MEM admin center.

Device restriction profiles

Need to lock down devices for security? Perhaps you want to block the TikTok app? If you want to 'turn things off' then the chances are you will need to create device restriction profiles. The available settings are broad, with each platform having a different set of available restrictions. Here are a few commonly configured restrictions:

- Set password minimum length on mobile devices.
- Block screen capture on iOS devices.
- Require encryption on macOS devices.
- Turn on Microsoft Defender SmartScreen for Windows 10 devices.
- Set the maintenance window hours for Windows 10 Surface Hub devices.

Do it – Build your own device restriction profile

1. Sign in to the MEM admin center and go to *Devices > Configuration profiles*.
2. Select *Create Profile*.
3. Walk through the Create wizard for a device restriction profile on each platform.

Choose a suitable name and description and then explore the available settings for the platform.

4. Optionally, assign the profile to a group of users or devices and see the resulting configuration on a test device.

Device features

The Device features profile type is only used for Apple devices (iOS and macOS). It contains a group of settings used to configure different aspects of the OS or the platform itself. For example, you could configure the home screen layout, set up AirPrint, Single Sign-On or set a custom wallpaper. Here are a few common examples of device feature profile usage:

*   Set AirPrint destination printers by network address for iOS devices.

*   Configure notification settings for corporate-owned iOS devices.

*   Set the iOS home screen layout and add app icons to the dock.

*   Hide a list of authorized local users from the login screen for macOS devices.

    To see the full list of device feature settings, see Microsoft docs: http://bit.ly/2L87su2.

Email

The email profile bucket is for setting up the "built-in" email client for each platform. For iOS and Windows 10 that is the 'Mail" app and for Android you get a choice of configuring Gmail or another commonly used third-party mail app called "Nine for work". My advice is to leave these mail profiles alone and instead deploy the Outlook mail app. It will allow much more control over mail app settings and data protection. We will cover app configuration in Chapter 7 and app protection in Chapter 8. You can find the full list of email settings in Microsoft docs: http://bit.ly/37Xw55R.

Resource access (Wi-Fi, wired, VPN and certificates)

If you need devices to connect seamlessly to wireless networks or be able to spin up a Virtual Private Network (VPN) to tunnel back through your on-prem VPN server, you'll need resource access profiles. Amongst customers, the most configured profile type is certificates. The reason is that certificates are a building block for several other profile types and these profiles are chained together – most enterprise Wi-Fi and VPN configurations authenticate with certificates so first you deploy the certificate profile and then you reference that certificate in a Wi-Fi or VPN profile.

Certificate profiles

In MEM there are two general 'types' of certificates issued to managed devices: trusted and generated certificates.

Trusted certificates – These are exported from your organization's existing root Certificate Authority in a .cer format and then uploaded to MEM in the form of a Trusted Certificate Profile. Each device that you deploy the profile to will download exactly the same trusted certificate – it is not unique per device.

Generated certificates – These are unique, per device or user certificates generated and issued to devices on-the-fly. To configure a managed device to ask for one of these unique certificates you create either a PKCS certificate profile or a SCEP certificate profile and deploy it to the device. In addition to creating the profile, you will also need to configure certificate issuing infrastructure or connectors to third-party cloud services to do that.

Wi-Fi profiles

Wi-Fi profiles save you the pain of handing out the SSID and password to users on post-it notes or putting it on posters around the office. Once you create and deploy a profile, users will automatically be connected to your on-prem Wi-Fi network.

When configuring a profile for Wi-Fi you have two options: Basic and Enterprise.

If your network infrastructure is enterprise-grade then you will almost always choose Enterprise. Although it's more complex to set up, it is undoubtedly more secure.

VPN profiles

MEM supports creating and deploying VPN profiles from all the major VPN providers including CheckPoint, Cisco, SonicWall, F5 Palo Alto, Pulse Secure, Citrix, Zcaler and Netmotio. MEM also provides a dedicated VPN profile type for its own new-to-market VPN server called "Microsoft Tunnel". If your organization uses an unlisted VPN product, don't worry – it is also possible to create a "Custom VPN" profile.

Windows 10-specific profiles

The following configuration profile types are just for Windows 10 devices:

Delivery Optimization

Delivery Optimization is a Windows 10 feature that allows certain downloads to be more efficient by getting content from peers or caching servers on the same local network rather than reaching out to the internet. There is a lot of tuning that you can do, and MEM provides first-class configuration experiences for the delivery optimization engine. Delivery optimization settings become very handy when you deploy Windows updates or large Win32 applications.

Device Firmware Configuration Interface (DFCI)

DFCI is a new technology that allows you to configure the BIOS settings remotely and securely. If you are using devices that support DFCI, you can specify settings to disable hardware components (for example, turning off the camera at the BIOS level in highly secure locations) or lock the ability for end-users to mess with the BIOS settings at all. At the time of writing this, DFCI is supported on just the Microsoft Surface device lineup (Surface Pro 7, Pro X, Laptop 3, Book 3, Laptop Go) but you can expect it to become more popular on other devices in the future.

Windows 10 Team Device Restrictions (Surface Hub Settings)

Surface Hub devices (the big digital whiteboards) run an OS called Windows 10 Team. That OS has an MDM stack (Configuration Service Providers or CSP's) that is slightly different from the everyday Windows 10 desktop editions. For example, there are settings for controlling welcome screens, proximity sensors and customizing meeting experiences. That means you should only use this profile if you need to manage and customize experiences on hubs.

Identity Protection (Windows Hello for Business settings)

Sign in to Windows without passwords! Windows Hello for Business is a password replacement technology where you can use biometrics (your face) or a PIN for signing into Windows and then authenticating to other resources. MEM has a first-class profile type for pushing down the Windows Hello for Business settings.

> Identity Protection profile types overlap with the broad, tenant-wide configuration for Windows Hello that is available in the *Devices > Enroll devices > Windows enrollment > Windows Hello for Business* section of the MEM portal.

To read more about the infrastructure you will need for Windows Hello for Business, beyond just deploying a profile and getting this to work end-to-end, see my blog post on the topic – http://bit.ly/3aWzTGb.

Kiosk

Windows 10 devices can be locked down into a single- or multi-app kiosk mode. A single-app kiosk is a fully locked down, limited user experience that only runs one app, and that app needs to be a Windows 10 UWP app (aka Modern app) from the Microsoft store. The Multi-app kiosk is a bit more flexible in that you can hand-pick a selection of Win32 and UWP apps and allow end-users a Start menu to jump between them. Multi-App Kiosk profiles let you define the apps and browsers that are allowed. You can define the apps using a unique Application User Model ID (AUMID) and define a custom start and taskbar layout for the kiosk.

> ### Tip! – Find the AUMID for a Windows app
>
> AUMID's are just a unique app identifier and all apps in Windows have them. You can use File Explorer, Windows Registry or PowerShell to find it. See this doc to learn how: http://bit.ly/3aZpeL1.

Secure Assessment (Take a test)

"Take a test" is a neat little feature built into Windows 10 and used by education institutions. The Secure Assessment profile allows you to turn it on and configure the settings. The feature locks down a PC so that students can only use it for sitting a given exam and don't have access to anything they shouldn't. Read more about Secure Assessment configuration on Microsoft docs: http://bit.ly/3841FPn.

Shared Multi-User device

This profile exists to configure the Windows 10 settings from the Shared PC Configuration Service Provider (CSP). If you have a device used by many users (for example, in a classroom or call center), you should look at this profile type. You will find it useful for cleaning up stale user profiles or configuring power settings. This profile type is often used by schools when locking down computers because it allows you to remove access to the local hard drive and have users save everything to the cloud.

Administrative templates

If you are a fan of old-school Group Policy, then this section is for you. Administrative Templates are a relatively new way of accessing thousands of Group Policy settings from the MEM console and delivering them over the MDM channel instead of via the traditional 'on-prem only' Group Policy and domain controller channel. MEM does this by ingesting a series of Group Policy Administrative Template (.admx) files into the cloud and exposing each setting within them to you in MEM. Not only can you see Windows 10 settings but you can also configure settings for Edge, Office and third-party apps.

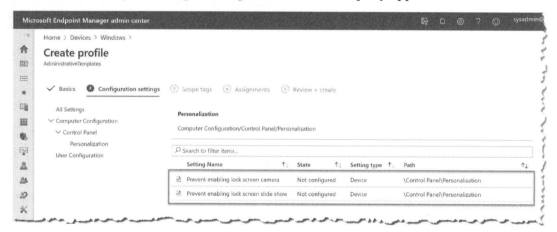

Group Policy analytics

Are you migrating from Group Policy to MDM for Windows 10 management? Group Policy analytics is a tool that can help you with that process. It involves you jumping on one of your domain controllers in your on-prem environment and exporting each Group Policy Object (GPO) that you have in place for your Windows 10 devices. You upload each of those GPO's into MEM which then compares what you have in those GPO's versus the settings available to be configured via MDM.

The output is a report for each GPO showing how supported the GPO is in MDM – a percentage of supported settings. You can then drill into settings that are not supported in MDM to understand if these are even needed anymore. I guarantee there are some old Internet Explorer 8 settings in there just waiting to be spring-cleaned!

Custom

Custom settings are a catch-all for any settings that you can't find anywhere in the MEM admin center. These are settings supported by the platform you manage but without an appropriate first-class configuration interface. To write custom settings you first need to make sure the platform you are trying to configure supports the setting, then you need to learn the custom setting format (which is different per platform). Windows 10 and Android take OMA-URI format for input and Apple uses a proprietary format that you get when you export from Apple Configurator and Apple policy manager tools.

Windows 10

You've searched the console up and down and still can't find the setting you're looking for. This sometimes happens when a new version of Windows 10 is released with new features but MEM hasn't caught up. The next step is to brush up on the Windows 10 Configuration Service Provider (CSP) documentation. Remember, CSP's are just the bits of code that exist on PC's that know how to convert management commands into actions. The Windows 10 CSP reference contains a list of every CSP in Windows and how to use it. The reference also contains information about the supported Windows editions for settings (this is important because there are a bunch that can't be messed with on Windows 10 home).

The easiest way I have found to use the CSP reference is to search for a setting name from the overview page. You can find the Windows 10 CSP reference on Microsoft docs: https://bit.ly/2QUfSVu.

Android

Android custom policies are very rare. At the time of writing this there are only three settings supported for the Android Enterprise work profile. In the rare case that you need custom settings for Android your course of action is to head to the Microsoft docs page where you can copy and paste the example OMA-URI: https://bit.ly/31TIrIZ.

iOS/iPadOS and macOS

If you have a tough time finding a specific setting in MEM for iOS or macOS devices your first step (after searching the Microsoft documentation) is to see if it is even an MDM configurable setting. You can do that by reading up on Apple's latest configuration profile reference or downloading Apple Configurator and browsing a list of configuration profile settings. Once you find the setting in Configurator, you can configure it the way you want and then export that configuration as a .mobileconfig file which can then be uploaded to the MEM admin center. You can find Apple's configuration profile reference here: https://apple.co/3jIIdKS.

Do it – Create a custom profile for Windows 10

In this exercise you will configure a custom policy for Windows 10 devices – the custom policy contains settings for enabling self-service password reset for users so that they can reset passwords from the Windows 10 lock screen.

1. Sign in to the MEM admin center and go to *Devices > Configuration profiles*.

2. Create a new profile for Windows 10 and select *Custom*.

3. Provide a name and description. For example:

  a. Name: Enable SSPR link.

  b. Description: This policy enables a Self-Service Password reset link from the lock screen.

4. Select *Next*.

5. On the *Configuration Settings* page, select *Add* and then type in the following custom setting details:

  a. Name: Add SSPR link.

  b. Description: Adds SSPR link to the lock screen.

  c. OMA-URI:

   ./Vendor/MSFT/Policy/Config/Authentication/AllowAadPasswordReset

  d. Data type: Integer

  e. Value: 1

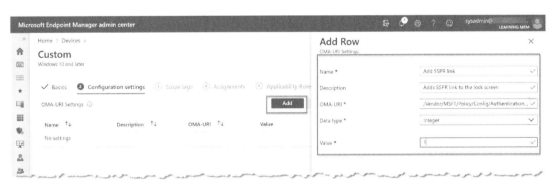

6. Complete the wizard steps and assign the policy to a group of test users or devices. After they check in they will apply the policy and show the password reset link.

This exercise was to get you familiar with creating custom policies. To make this SSPR link scenario work end-to-end there are some other requirements you'd need to configure outside of MEM. See the Microsoft docs page for the full details: http://bit.ly/3rIUx2I.

OEMConfig

Android is special because of the diversity of device manufacturers and models on which the OS is installed. Android devices are used so widely, on such a variety of devices – from mobile phones to barcode scanners to digital signage boards. Original Equipment Manufacturers (OEM's) build specialized devices with different hardware capabilities and characteristics and the Android operating system is not able to keep up with the constant innovation from each OEM and add it natively to the MDM stack.

Instead, the architecture for dealing with these special per-OEM settings is OEMConfig. When OEMs, for example Zebra or Honeywell, develop a new device and want the new device features to be configurable via MEM, they will develop Application Programming Interfaces (API's) on the device and a companion OEMConfig app. That app gets installed on the device and does all the heavy lifting when it comes to configuration. MEM's job is to give IT admins a console to configure the desired settings and push those settings down to the app on the device. The great thing about this architecture is that it enables MEM and other UEM products to always have the latest and greatest settings available to configure. When you set up a new OEMConfig profile in MEM, the console reaches out in real-time to a schema provided by the OEMConfig vendor so that the configuration options are always up to date with the latest settings.

Tip! – Check support for OEMConfig

You can find the list of supported OEMConfig apps for MEM on Microsoft docs: http://bit.ly/3pLZcyw.

Do it – Create an OEMConfig profile

In this exercise you will add an OEMConfig configuration to disable power saving mode on Zebra devices. This will require you to first obtain the OEMConfig app from the Google

Play Store, then create and deploy the custom OEMConfig policy.

1. In the MEM admin center, on the left navigation menu, go to *Apps > Android apps* and select *Add*.

2. Select *Managed Google Play app*.

3. On the Managed Google Play page, search for *Zebra OEMConfig*.

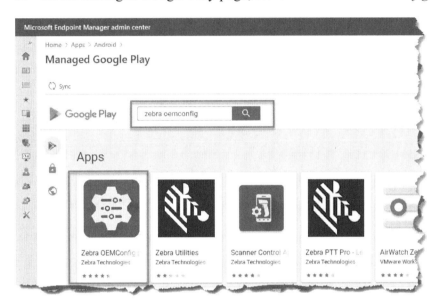

4. Select the tile for Zebra OEMConfig powered by MX app and approve it. Choose *Keep approved when app requests new permissions*.

5. Select the *Sync* button at the top left and return to the MEM apps list. Soon you will see the app appear in the list.

6. On the left navigation menu, go to *Devices > Configuration profiles > Create Profile*.

7. Select *Android Enterprise*, then *OEMConfig*.

8. Provide a name and description for the policy (e.g., Disable Power Saving mode. This policy configures Zebra devices to disable power-saving mode)

9. Select the *OEMConfig app* link and choose *Zebra OEMConfig powered by MX* from the list of OEMConfig apps. Select *Next*.

10. On the Configuration Settings page, select the *Locate* link to search for a setting. Search for *"Battery Saver Mode"* and then select it from the context pane. The entire Power Configuration options transaction step will be added to the configuration designer.

11. Locate the *Battery Saver Mode setting* and turn it off.

12. Browse and configure other settings available in the configuration designer by returning to the *Transaction step* tree node and selecting *Configure* for different categories of settings.

13. Select *Next* and optionally assign the policy to a group of managed Zebra devices and complete the OEMConfig policy configuration.

Tip! – Deploy the OEMConfig app to devices

Some OEM's ship their Android devices with the OEMConfig app already installed and others do not. Either way, I recommend deploying it in MEM just in case. This way, MEM will keep the app up to date with new features and settings as they are released by the OEM.

Windows update policies

MEM has two different policy types for deciding when and how Windows 10 devices should download and install operating system updates from the cloud. These are "Update rings" and "Feature Update" policies.

Update rings policy type has existed in MEM for a long time and is supported on Windows 10 versions 1607 and later. These profiles let you choose over 20 settings about the Windows 10 update experience on devices including the update servicing channel, maintenance hours and the notifications that users receive before a required reboot. You can use the "Rings" policy type to configure settings for both Feature updates (the major OS update event that happens twice a year for Windows 10) and quality updates (the bug fixes and security updates that Microsoft releases once a month).

The newer "Feature updates" profile type contains just one setting – you simply define what version of Windows your managed devices should be on and those devices will upgrade to that version and stay there. At the time of writing, Feature updates is a preview feature.

CHAPTER 6

CONFIGURING COMPLIANCE PROFILES AND SETTINGS

Compliance policies are a set of standards that you can define for which devices should compare themselves against. If the device cannot comply with any setting you defined in a compliance policy, it gets a big fat "Not compliant" stamp which has a series of implications for it later down the track.

Compliance policies

The distinction between compliance policy settings and configuration profile settings can sometimes be a difficult line to draw. It used to be true that configuration profiles applied settings to devices and compliance policies were just there to check if a setting is applied or not. The compliance policy's job was to mark the device as non-compliant until the user or admin resolved it. That is not true anymore. Compliance policies are platform specific and each platform has its own way of interpreting and enforcing the different settings available for configuration in a policy. For some compliance settings, MEM is not able to ask the device if a given setting is configured in a certain way and so the only way to know if a device is compliant or not is to physically set the configuration. Take PIN settings for example – if you set a device PIN for each supported platform (iOS, macOS, Windows 10 and Android), you'll find that iOS and Windows 10 are able to force the user to apply a device PIN but on Android, MEM will mark the device as non-compliant until this is resolved by the user.

The below table shows the currently available compliance policy settings across supported platforms:

Setting	Windows 10	iOS/iPadOS	macOS	Android (work profile)	Android (COPE, COBO)
Device Health					
Require BitLocker	Yes				
Require Secure Boot to be enabled on the device	Yes				
Require code integrity	Yes				
Block jailbroken devices		Yes			
Block rooted devices				Yes	
Require the device to be at or under the Device Threat Level		Secured, Low, Medium, High		Secured, Low, Medium, High	Secured, Low, Medium, High
Require system integrity protection			Yes		
Google Play Services is configured				Yes	
Up to date security provider				Yes	
SafetyNet device attestation				Check basic integrity, Check basic integrity & certified devices	Check basic integrity, Check basic integrity & certified devices
Configuration Manager Compliance					
Require device compliance from Configuration Manager	Yes				
Operating System Version					
Minimum OS version	Yes	Yes	Yes	Yes	Yes
Maximum OS version	Yes	Yes	Yes	Yes	Yes
Minimum OS version for mobile devices	Yes				
Maximum OS version for mobile devices	Yes				
Minimum OS build version		Yes	Yes		

Maximum OS build version		Yes	Yes		
Minimum security patch level				Yes	Yes
System Security					
Require a password to unlock mobile devices	Yes	Yes	Yes	Yes	Yes
Allow simple passwords	Yes	Yes	Yes		
Required password type	Numeric /Alphanumeric	Numeric / Alphanumeric	Numeric / Alphanumeric	Password required – no restrictions, Weak biometric, Numeric, Numeric complex, Alphabetic, Alphanumeric, Alphanumeric with symbols	Password required – no restrictions, Weak biometric, Numeric, Numeric complex, Alphabetic, Alphanumeric, Alphanumeric with symbols
Minimum password length	Yes	Yes	Yes	Yes	Yes
Number of non-alphanumeric characters in password		Yes	Yes		
Maximum minutes after screen lock before password is required		Immediately, 1 min – 4 hours			
Maximum minutes of inactivity before password is required	Yes	Immediately, 1–15 minutes	Immediately, 1–15 minutes	1 min to 8 hours	1 min to 8 hours
Password expiration (days)	Yes	Yes	Yes	Yes	Yes
Number of previous passwords to prevent reuse	Yes	Yes	Yes	Yes	Yes
Require password when device returns from idle state (Mobile and Holographic)	Yes				

Encryption					
Require encryption of data storage on a device	Yes	Yes	Yes	Yes	Yes
Device Security					
Require Firewall	Yes		Yes		
Block incoming connections			Yes		
Enable stealth mode			Yes		
Require Trusted Platform Module (TPM)	Yes				
Require Antivirus	Yes				
Require Antispyware	Yes				
Block apps from unknown sources				Yes	
Company Portal app runtime integrity				Yes	
Block USB debugging on device				Yes	
Minimum security patch level				Yes	
Microsoft Defender					
Require Microsoft Defender Antimalware	Yes				
Microsoft Defender Antimalware minimum version	Yes				
Require Microsoft Defender Antimalware security intelligence up to date	Yes				
Require Real-time protection	Yes				
Gatekeeper					
Allow apps downloaded from these locations			Mac App Store, Mac App Store and identified developers, Anywhere		

Microsoft Defender for Endpoint (MDE)					
Require the device to be at or under the machine risk score	Clear, Low, Medium, High			Clear, Low, Medium, High	Clear, Low, Medium, High
Email					
Unable to set up email on the device		Yes			
Restricted Apps					
Restricted Apps		Yes			

Do it – Create a compliance policy for each platform

1. In the MEM admin center, go to *Devices > Compliance policies*.

2. Select *Create Policy* and walk through creating a policy for each platform (Android Enterprise, iOS/iPadOS, macOS, Windows 10).

3. As a bonus step, assign the policy to a test user group and monitor the impact the policy has on the *Compliance* property for the device. You can see this by going to *Devices > All devices* in the Compliance column or by selecting the device and viewing the properties on the *Overview* page.

Tip! – What is the Built-in Device Compliance Policy I see in my device reports?

When viewing a single device to see what compliance policies have applied you may notice there is also a policy called "Built-in Device Compliance Policy" that you didn't create. This policy reflects the status of the tenant-wide compliance policy settings that are applied for all devices in the environment. Global compliance settings are discussed a little later in this chapter.

Device Health Attestation (DHA) for Windows 10 devices

Starting in Windows 10, Microsoft spun up a new security-based cloud service that is used to ensure strong, tamper-resistant health signals from the device to MEM and other UEM products. Each time a Windows 10 device boots, the OS itself gathers measurement signals from firmware components and UEFI so they can be measured against the last boot. The device automatically sends that data to the "Remote Health Attestation" cloud service which tells MEM if the device is healthy or not. This means that if you configure any of the "Windows Health Attestation Service evaluation rules", the device itself is not telling Intune if it complies with a policy, the remote health attestation service is doing it.

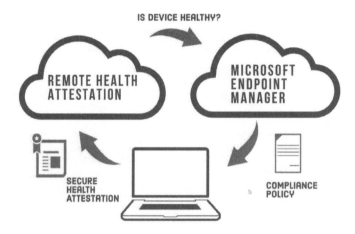

Configuration Manager compliance for Windows 10

When devices are co-managed you have the option to allow Configuration manager servers to update the compliance status of device objects in Intune. You do this by configuring the setting *"Require device compliance from Configuration Manager"*.

Before you start flicking this setting on, there are a few things to know. First, you will need to have enabled co-management (see Chapter 12). Second, you will need to have the

"Compliance" workload pointing to Configuration Manager. In this position, Configuration Manager will be the boss of compliance for your co-managed devices and tell Intune if they should be marked as compliant or not. The advantage of adding compliance signals from Configuration Manager servers is access to a lot more compliance settings exposed through *configuration items* and *baselines* features in Configuration Manager.

Global compliance settings

The following settings affect your entire MEM account and cannot be individually targeted to groups.

Mark devices with no compliance policy as Compliant/Not compliant

This setting can be used to really dial up the security in your tenant. People tend to start turning this on when they are also using Conditional Access policies (covered in Chapter 11). The default setting is "Compliant", which means that if you forgot to target some devices with a policy, they would be marked as compliant and not blocked by device-based Conditional Access. If you flick the default to say that devices are "Not compliant" until proven otherwise you should be careful to make sure all devices are targeted with a relevant policy.

Enhanced jailbreak detection

Although this is a global compliance setting, it's only used for iOS and iPadOS devices. The feature allows the OS itself to use location services to better detect jailbreaks when a big change of location is detected in a small amount of time. Since it uses location services you should consider a few things before turning this on. Firstly, sending location data more often will affect device battery life. Second, users must enable the location services themselves – if they don't, the device will be marked non-compliant.

Compliance status validity period (days)

Do you have devices that you enroll and then shove in a spare locker? You will want to pay attention to this global setting. It keeps an eye on how long since the devices last checked in with MEM. If they go missing in action, they will be marked as Not compliant.

You can tell a device was marked "Not compliant" because of this global setting when you start looking at reports for individual devices. Each of these global settings appears in a policy applied to all devices called *Built-in Device Compliance Policy* and this setting is denoted by the *is active* setting.

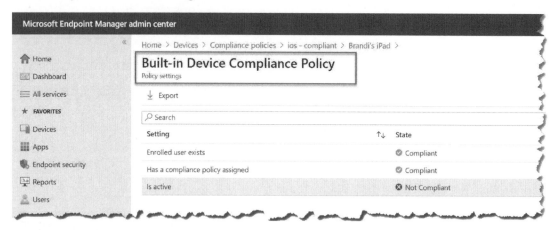

Notifications and actions for non-compliant devices

Instead of making devices report themselves as "Not compliant" straight away, you can send notifications to give users on enrolled devices subtle nudges to make the required changes on their own. The idea is that you layer these actions into a compliance schedule. For example, you could give users a week to fix compliance on their own. If devices are still not compliant after a week you could have MEM automatically send them an email or app notification in the Company Portal. Finally, after another week of grace, you could have MEM mark the device as "Not compliant", which has implications for Conditional Access that we will discuss further in Chapter 11.

The following non-compliance actions are supported for each platform:

	Windows 10	iOS/iPadOS	macOS	Android (work profile)	Android (COPE, COBO)
Mark device non-compliant	Yes	Yes	Yes	Yes	Yes
Send email to end-user	Yes	Yes	Yes	Yes	Yes
Send push notification to end-user	No	Yes	No	Yes	Yes
Remotely lock the device	Yes	Yes	Yes	Yes	Yes
Retire the device	No	Yes	Yes	Yes	Yes

When using the "Send email to end-user" action, you can customize one or more email templates, including company branding information, email subject and body. You can also add a localized message for each region where devices are managed.

Do it – Try out compliance notifications

1. Go to the MEM admin center and choose *Devices > Compliance policies > Notifications*.

2. Select *Create Notification*.

3. Provide a name for the notification (e.g., 1st warning for non-compliant device) and customize the email header and footer configuration and branding. Then select *Next*.

4. On the *Notification message templates* page, add a custom notification message including an email subject and body that will be sent to users on their first warning. You can optionally add messages for users in other regions (languages).

5. Complete the wizard steps, then review one of your previously created compliance policies and go to the *Properties* page.

6. Select the *Edit* link next to *Actions for noncompliance*.

7. On the *Actions for noncompliance* page, add a new action of *Send email to end-user*, then choose the message template that you just created.

8. Review and save the configuration.

As a bonus step, re-order the schedule so that users first receive the email message (after 0 days) and then the device is marked as non-compliant after 7 days. Experiment with additional device actions such as "Retire the non-compliant device", "Send push notification to end-user" and "remotely lock the non-compliant device". If you want to implement several instances of the same action on different schedules, that is possible, too.

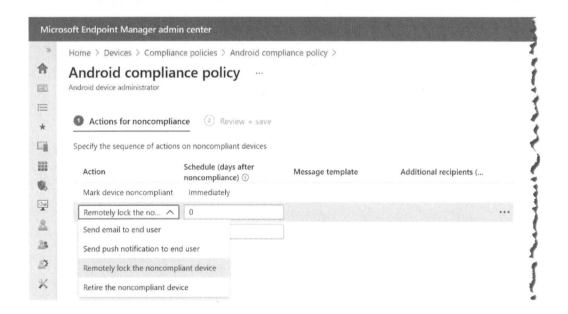

Integrating with Mobile Threat Defense (MTD) services

Mobile Threat Defense (MTD) (also known as Mobile Threat Management (MTM) or Mobile Threat Protection (MTP)) products are just security products that specialize in mobile device platforms. They provide several security features that are typically not provided by UEM's like MEM. For example, they can be used for detecting malware in mobile apps or dodgy app-signers. MEM allows you to integrate with MTD Partners to help calculate overall device compliance. This means that in addition to all the configurable compliance settings, you can have the MTD product send MEM a "Risk score" for the device based on its own calculations. You enable this risk score to be factored in by toggling *"Require the device to be at or under the Device Threat Level"* on and setting up the backend so that the MTD partner can securely communicate this information to MEM.

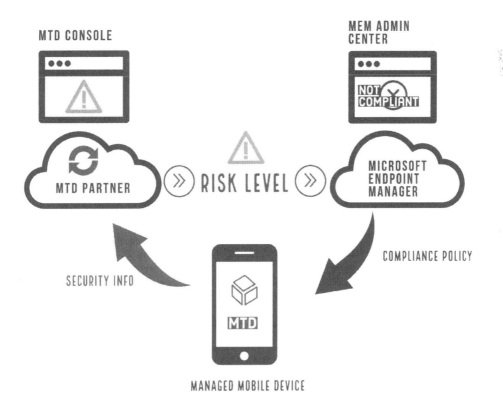

MEM currently supports the following MTD partners for compliance integration:

- Lookout for Work
- Symantec Endpoint Protection Mobile

- Check Point SandBlast Mobile

- Zimperium

- Pradeo

- Better Mobile

- Sophos Mobile

- Wandera Mobile Threat Defense

Since more partners are being integrated daily, I recommend checking this Microsoft docs page for the latest updated list: https://bit.ly/32iCO7u.

Microsoft Defender for Endpoint (MDE)

Instead of using and paying for a third-party product from the list above, you have the option to integrate Microsoft Defender for Endpoint (MDE), which you already have licenses for if you opted for either Microsoft 365 E5 or EMS E5 subscriptions. At the time of writing this book, Defender is available to provide compliance and health signals for both Windows 10 and Android compliance policies but not iOS.

Compliance policies in the big picture of Conditional Access (CA)

Before wrapping up this compliance chapter, it's important that I briefly cover how compliance rolls up to the bigger picture for security – Conditional Access (CA). Conditional Access is a big engine where you can set the rules (conditions) for when people try to access any corporate content. In short, conditional access can look at all the conditions under which a user is trying to access a resource and then decide what to do about it. One of the rules that you can define is that "Devices must be compliant" to access corporate stuff. This is where MEM Compliance and specifically compliance policies come into play – the device's compliance state, as computed by MEM, is pumped into the overall Conditional Access check. We will go much deeper on CA in Chapter 11

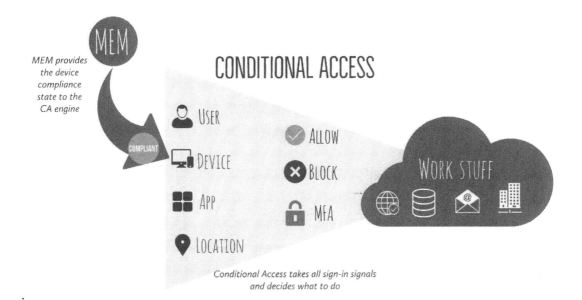

CHAPTER 7

CONFIGURING ENDPOINT SECURITY

In this chapter we're going to focus on the Endpoint Security node of the MEM console. You'll get a good understanding of each of the security-based workloads and learn about the integration with broader Microsoft security features such as Microsoft Defender for Endpoint (MDE).

Overview of Endpoint Security

The Endpoint Security node of the MEM console is a carved-out section containing all the things that an endpoint security expert needs. Microsoft recognized that in many organizations, there was often a different team of IT admins with a highly specialized set of skills who were in charge of managing security all-up across the company's devices.

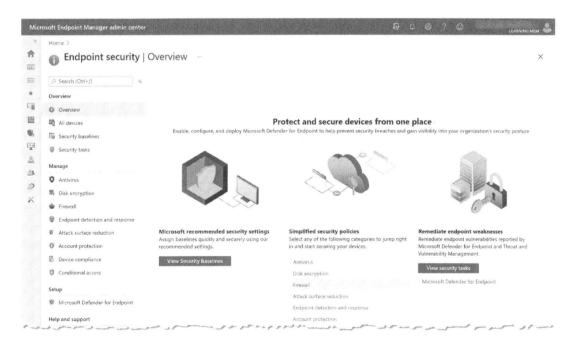

Those security experts have no business in setting up device enrollment or deploying apps to desktops and they certainly don't care for configuring iOS wallpapers – what they really need is their own console within the admin center focused on the security tasks they perform daily. For this reason, you will see some overlap with policies – some features have an entry point from multiple places in the admin center and some settings exist across multiple profile types.

Tip! – As a general practice you should use the Security node as the default place to configure anything security related instead of using the profiles available in the Configuration profiles section.

Security baselines for Windows 10

In my previous role at Microsoft as a field engineer, I'd help customers create a secure but productive Windows desktop experience for their users by configuring Group Policy settings the right way. The thing that made this task easier was the fact that we did not have to start from scratch. Security experts in the industry (both Microsoft and other organizations) created Security Baselines. These baseline Group Policy Objects (GPO's) were a secure starting point for configuring Windows 10. The benefit of baselines is that security experts can do all the analysis of the most secure (but usable) configurations, bundle them up and share them for general use. Microsoft publishes GPO security baselines with each release of Windows and then other organizations, such as the Defense Information Systems Agency (DISA), would derive their own based on their security research, which could then be adopted by government organizations.

In the world of MDM and cloud management, baselines have re-emerged as a crucial tool for Windows 10 management. At the time of writing this book, the following baselines are available in the MEM admin center:

- Windows 10 Security Baselines

- Microsoft Defender for Endpoint (MDE) Baselines

- Microsoft Edge Baseline

Here's the basic flow for deploying baselines:

1. Choose one of the baselines (Windows 10, MDE or Edge).

2. Create a new profile. That profile will be pre-configured with all the settings from the latest version of the Microsoft-provided baseline. You can customize these settings to your liking to make them more or less strict.

3. Deploy it to devices.

Windows 10 gets updated twice a year so you can expect that there will be new Windows features coming out with new security settings. Microsoft publishes a new baseline version into the MEM console to keep up with these changes and you can update your deployed profile to include any changes in the new baseline.

Tip! – Test first!

Security baselines include security settings that are aimed at 'hardening' (restricting) devices so I recommend thoroughly testing with a pilot of test devices first. Once you've validated that all your apps are working and the device is functioning as expected, you can deploy it broadly.

Do it – Try out Security baselines

1. Go to the MEM admin center and sign in.

2. Navigate to *Endpoint Security > Security baselines*. Select *Windows 10 Security Baseline*.

3. Select *Create Profile*. On the *Basics* page, add a name and description for the profile. (e.g., Security baseline for Win10 devices in the US).

4. On the *Configuration Settings* screen you will see all settings that are defined in the baseline and their recommended value.

5. Locate the *Block Password Manager* setting and select *Not Configured*.

6. Complete the creation and, optionally, the assignment steps.

Tip! – Export baselines

You can export your new security baseline into a .CSV file to help with any documentation. You can also choose to update the settings in your baselines based on updated guidance from Microsoft when new baselines come out. To do that, select your customized baseline, then *Change version* from the action bar. You'll then be able to choose to overwrite your customized settings with Microsoft recommendations or keep your own.

Antivirus policy

Antivirus profile types in the Endpoint Security node are there to tweak the Microsoft Defender Antivirus settings on managed devices. For Windows 10, Defender is integrated into the OS and labeled as *Virus and threat protection settings* and you do not need to do anything special to prepare the devices to start using this profile type. On macOS, however, you will need to get the Microsoft Defender for Endpoint agent installed first.

The following Antivirus profile types are available for configuration:

- Microsoft Defender Antivirus exclusions (Windows 10)

- Microsoft Defender Antivirus (Windows 10)

- Windows Security experience (Windows 10)

- Antivirus (macOS)

Deploy antivirus configuration for Servers (integration with Configuration Manager)

Server Management? I'm not kidding. You can use MEM to configure the bulk of security settings on servers even though servers can't be enrolled into MDM. This is all made possible with the integration between the on-prem Configuration Manager product and Intune. Before you can deploy this type of profile, there's some setup work. Specifically, you need to enable "Tenant attach" (which we'll cover in-depth in Chapter 12).

The below diagram shows the high-level architecture for deploying Antivirus policies to servers.

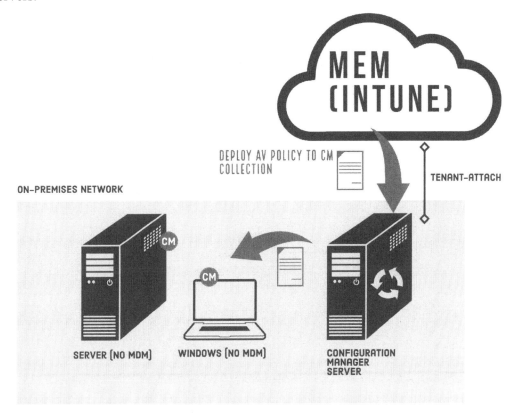

Do it – Deploy Antivirus Settings to MDM devices

1. Go to the MEM admin center, then *Endpoint Security > Antivirus*.

2. Try creating each of the different policy types across macOS and Windows 10.

3. Optionally, assign the profiles to groups of users and make sure the settings were applied successfully.

Disk encryption policy

Endpoint Protection disk encryption policies help you protect data on both macOS and Windows 10 PC's in case they are ever lost or stolen. Microsoft BitLocker (for Windows 10) and FileVault (for macOS) provide full disk encryption and the settings for both encryption and recovery can be tweaked to find the right balance between security and usability in your organization. Encryption keys are also backed up to MEM so if a user is ever locked out of their device, a helpdesk professional or the user can retrieve the keys.

Do it – Try out encryption settings

1. Go to the MEM admin center, then *Endpoint Security > Disk encryption*.

2. Try creating both a BitLocker and FileVault policy.

3. Optionally, assign the profiles to groups of users and make sure the settings were applied successfully.

Tip! – Enable virtual TPM on test devices

If you are testing security settings such as BitLocker on Hyper-V VM's you should make sure the VM is enabled with a "Virtual TPM". The *Enable Trusted Platform module* option in the VM Settings, under security, will achieve that.

Firewall policy

I've never seen an enterprise desktop environment that didn't need to centrally manage and configure some client firewall exclusions. The firewall policy type allows you to both apply broad-stroke configurations, like turning the firewall on/off, and go super deep with specific firewall rules. Like encryption profiles, firewall profiles work by applying configuration to the built-in firewall component of each operating system – Windows 10 has the *Network and Firewall security settings* components of Windows 10 and macOS uses the application firewall.

Do it – Try out Firewall settings

1. Go to the MEM admin center, then *Endpoint Security > Firewall*.

2. Try creating a Firewall policy for both Windows 10 and macOS.

3. Optionally, assign the profiles to groups of users and make sure the settings were applied successfully. Note: before you can try out the *Microsoft Defender Firewall (ConfigMgr)* profile type you will need to have set up tenant attach, which is covered in Chapter 12).

Attack Surface Reduction (ASR) for Windows 10

ASR is a security feature of Windows 10. Security attacks are typically by a known set of attack vectors, and this security feature lets you implement some common mitigations to shut the door on those vectors. It's kind of like when I'm working at home and my dog jumps up on door handles to open the door and interrupt my meetings – I swapped out the door handle with the ball type that the dog can't turn with her paws.

Detailed information on implementing ASR on Windows 10 is outside the scope of this book, but I'll provide a quick overview of each of the profile types and point you to the Windows Security documentation to learn more.

- **Device control** – Block access from external devices like Bluetooth and removable drives.

- **Attack surface reduction rules** – Block scripts and Office macros.

- **App and browser isolation** – Enables *Application Guard* in the Edge browser. This Windows 10 feature can put browser sessions into a temporary virtual bubble when a potentially malicious website is reached – the browser then won't be able to access anything else on the system.

- **Exploit protection** – Allows you to enable a known set of exploit protection rules. These rules were first introduced to Windows 7 as EMET (Enhanced Mitigation Experience Toolkit) and later built into Windows 10 as *Exploit Guard* (later re-named *Exploit protection)*.

- **Web protection** – Enable Microsoft Defender's web content filter or enforce Windows SmartScreen, which maintains a list of known bad URL's – or executable files coming from those URL's – and verifies before launching them.

- **Application control** – This security feature is a cousin of Microsoft's *AppLocker* which has been part of the operating system since Windows 7. You can lock down Windows 10 into a secure state by only allowing code that is signed (or an exception that you define) to run. This feature used to be called *Device Guard – Configurable Code Integrity*.

Do it – Try out ASR policies

1. Go to the MEM admin center, then *Endpoint Security > Attack surface reduction*.

2. Try out a few different ASR profile types. I recommend something easy such as the *Device control* profile with the *Block removable storage* setting enabled.

3. Optionally, assign the profiles to groups of users and make sure the settings were applied successfully.

Account protection policy for Windows 10

The Account protection policy type includes configuration of settings that protect user accounts and identities. This includes Windows Hello for business and Credential Guard settings. Windows Hello controls the end-user Windows authentication experience (allowing the PC to be unlocked with a PIN or biometric credentials like a face), and Credential guard is a way of hardening user authentication processes by popping the main process (LSASS) into a virtualized container. These security settings are pretty involved when it comes to requirements and setup, so I recommend having a good read of the Microsoft security documentation before deploying these profiles with MEM.

- Credential Guard overview – http://bit.ly/2JXPAC1.
- Windows Hello for Business overview – http://bit.ly/3hZpQ50.

Microsoft Defender for Endpoint integration and Endpoint detection and response policy

Microsoft Defender for Endpoint (MDE) is the premium endpoint security offering for Windows 10. It's available with any of the Windows 10 premium (level 5) licensing plans, which you can test out via a trial.

The premium licensing gives you access to a combination of Windows 10 Security features, cloud services and a managed service where remote security experts sitting in a Microsoft Security Operations Center (SOC) can help you respond to security incidents within your environment.

> **Tip! – Microsoft product name changes**
>
> At the time of writing this book, the product name had only just changed from *Microsoft Defender Advanced Threat Detection (MDATP)* to *Microsoft Defender for Endpoint (MDE)*. A lot of Microsoft documentation and portal pages still use the old name. If you see the "MDATP" or "ATP" terminology used anywhere you can assume it should say "MDE".

MDE is integrated into the MEM Admin center and enables seamless onboarding of MEM devices to the MDE service. You can initiate this connection using two types of *Endpoint Protection and Response* profiles:

- **Windows 10 and later – Endpoint detection and response (MDM)** – In this configuration profile you'll provide a special onboarding package that is unique to your environment. MEM will deliver this down to enrolled devices over the MDM channel which will activate a built-in (Sense) agent that can start communicating with the MDE service and sending important information about security threats on the device.

- **Windows 10 and Windows Server – Endpoint detection and response (ConfigMgr)** – Similar to Firewall and Encryption settings, devices that are not enrolled into MDM can still receive onboarding policy via integration with Configuration Manager. The contents of this profile are the same as the MDM type, but the delivery mechanism is different. For this profile, you push it to a ConfigMgr collection of devices (see Chapter 12 for more details on setting up "tenant attach", which is the basic requirement for delivering policies via on-prem configuration manager servers).

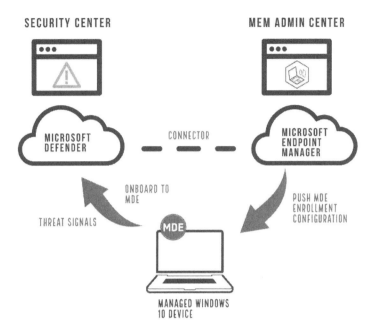

Do it – Try out MDE integration

In this exercise you will set up a connector between MDE and MEM. We'll then deploy an onboarding profile to Windows 10 MDM-enrolled devices so that they enroll in MDE service and start sending security information. For this exercise you will need to ensure you have trial licenses that include usage rights for MDE (such as the recommended Microsoft 365 E5 license).

1. Go to the MEM admin center, then navigate to *Endpoint Security > Microsoft Defender for Endpoint*.
2. Review the three steps for setup. Click the link on step 1, which will open a new web page for the Microsoft Defender Security Center (https://securitycenter.windows.com) advanced settings page. Note: on your first-ever use of the Microsoft Defender Security Center you may be prompted to enable the trial, even if you have assigned users with the correct Microsoft 365 E5 licenses. If this happens, follow the basic steps to sign up for the trial so that you can access the security center.

147

3. Locate the configuration setting *Microsoft Intune connection* and enable it.

4. Keep the Microsoft Defender Security Center tab open but return to the MEM admin center tab and refresh the page. You will eventually see the Connection status appear.

5. Now go to *Endpoint detection and response* on the left navigation pane and create a new *Endpoint detection and response (MDM)* policy for Windows 10.

6. On the *Configuration settings page* change the *Microsoft Defender for Endpoint client configuration package type* to *Onboarding blob*.

7. Now choose *Select onboarding file*.

8. Return to the Microsoft Defender Security Center and use the settings navigation menu to locate *Device management > Onboarding*.

9. Select *Mobile Device Management >Microsoft Intune* from the *Deployment method* dropdown and then choose *Download package*.

10. Save the .zip file locally on your management PC and then extract the "WindowsDefenderATP.onboarding" file.

11. Head back to the MEM browser tab and upload that file.

12. Assign the Endpoint detection and response profile to a group of Windows 10 PC's.

13. Once the devices have checked in and onboarded successfully, you can return to the Microsoft Defender Security Center. You will see each of the onboarded devices appear under the *Device inventory* page.

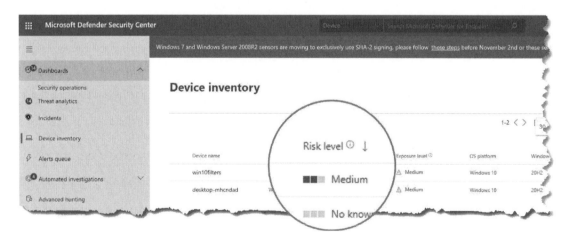

Security Tasks

Do you have a Security Operations (SecOps) team in your organization? They are the ones monitoring the environment for security issues and responding to the current threat landscape in the security world. They use hundreds of different tools for that, but if your company is all-in on the Microsoft 365 vision, chances are that your SecOps team is using Microsoft Defender for Endpoint (MDE). If so, that is great news for you because both your security and admin teams will benefit from this feature.

The concept is that Security "Operations" and "Administration" teams are usually different, located in different facilities, using different tools and do not communicate changes to endpoints well enough even though there is a lot of overlap between the work they do. Security Tasks is a feature that can help bridge that gap. In the Microsoft Defender Security Center (https://securitycenter.microsoft.com), active risks and threats are surfaced to the SecOps administrator who will perform some initial analysis. If the threat is something that a MEM admin needs to take care of (for example, removing a dodgy version of an app from some PC's remotely) the SecOps professional can create a new security task. The MEM admin can see this task, acknowledge it, do the required work and then close it and get on with her day.

Do it – Try out Security tasks

1. Sign in to the SecOps portal (The Microsoft Defender Security Center – https://Securitycenter.windows.com)

2. Use the left navigation bar to go to the *Threat & Vulnerability Management dashboard*.

3. On the dashboard page you will notice a *Top security recommendations* section on the right. If you have devices enrolled into MDE, some of these recommendations will show you impacted devices that require a software update.

4. Select the recommendation, then select *Remediation options*.

5. On this page you can add a description for the remediation task and set a completion date. To send this remediation to MEM Security admins, select *Open a ticket in Microsoft Endpoint Manager (for AAD joined devices)*.

6. Now return to the MEM admin center and navigate to *Endpoint Security > Security tasks*.

7. You will see the new task awaiting action, along with the remediation steps. You can optionally mark it as complete when you are finished making the required change in MEM.

CHAPTER 8

DEPLOYING APPS

In this chapter you will learn everything you need to know about App deployment with MEM. We will cover different types of apps and enterprise app programs such as Apple's Volume Purchase Program (VPP). In Chapters 9 and 10 we will dive deeper into other parts of the application lifecycle such as configuring the apps you deployed.

Overview of app types

There are over 30 "types" of apps that can be deployed with MEM. These can be loosely summarized into the following categories:

- **Store apps** – The publicly available consumer stores – Apple App store, Google Play Store and Microsoft Store.

- **Enterprise store apps** – App stores that are only accessible for organizations – Apple's Volume Purchase Program (VPP), Google's Managed Google Play (MGP) and Microsoft Store for Business (MSFB).

- **Line-of-business (LOB) apps** – Bring your own packaged apps – Apple .ipa files, Google .apk files and multiple supported file formats in Windows.

- **Microsoft first-party apps** – Special MEM integrations with Microsoft Office, Edge browser and Microsoft Defender for Endpoint.

- **Built-in apps** – Special MEM integrations for commonly used mobile applications that are needed for deploying app configuration policies including app protection policies.

- **Web links** – URL to any website. These can also come from special integration with Azure AD's web apps.

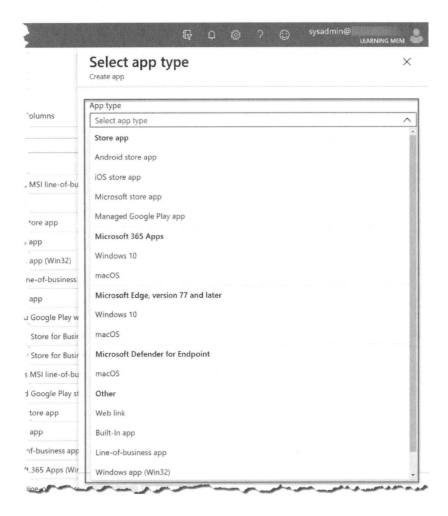

Note that the "Add app" menu in the MEM admin center does not have all 30 app types in it. You will learn in this section that some apps are automatically populated into your MEM environment via up-stream connectors and tokens with other Microsoft and third-party services.

iOS/iPadOS app types:

- **iOS store app** – One of the most popular app types deployed in MEM. Creating a store app in the MEM admin center is a very slick admin experience, too. The Apple App Store has an API that MEM can search directly from the admin center and add any available store app that you want to MEM, ready for assignment. To install store apps on managed devices requires that the user has signed into the Apple App Store with an Apple ID.

- **iOS Volume Purchase Program app** – Apple's Volume Purchase Program (VPP) allows companies and schools to buy multiple copies of paid apps from the store ready for deployment with MEM. It involves a two-step process where step 1 is to acquire the App from Apple VPP, then when the app is synced to MEM it will show up in the iOS app list and be ready for assignment. VPP apps offer a better user experience on devices because they don't prompt the user for an Apple ID.

- **iOS line-of-business (LOB) app** – LOB apps for iOS and iPadOS can be any app with .ipa file format. Typically, these are specialized apps developed in-house for a specific purpose.

- **Web link** – Any website can be deployed as a MEM web link; just enter a URL. On iOS, these apps, when deployed to iPads or iPhones, result in a tile on the homepage and are known as "web clips".

- **Built-in app** – These are a MEM-curated list of iOS store apps. The special thing about these apps is that they can be used with MEM's app protection policies, which we will cover in Chapter 9.

- **Managed iOS store app (deprecated)** – This app type is no longer used – it was replaced by Built-in apps.

- **Managed iOS line-of-business app (deprecated)** – This app type is no longer used – it was replaced by Built-in apps.

macOS app types:

- **macOS line-of-business (LOB) app** – Upload an in-house or third-party developed app for deployment. You must prepare macOS apps first – converting them from .pkg file format to the MEM-specific .intunemac format. If you have macOS apps with other formats such as .dmg you can convert those as well, but it takes a few steps – you must use other tools to convert to .pkg first.

- **Microsoft Edge (macOS)** – Microsoft's first-party browser is not really a different "App type", however the MEM admin center has a super simple experience for creating a package and deploying it to managed macOS devices.

- **Microsoft Defender for Endpoint (macOS)** – This app type has a super simple deployment experience for getting the MDE client installed on managed macOS devices.

- **Microsoft 365 Apps for Enterprise** – Deploy the suite of office apps to managed Macs including Word, Excel, PowerPoint, Outlook, OneNote, and Teams.

- **macOS Volume Purchase Program (VPP) app** – macOS apps (like iOS apps) can be bought in advance by schools and companies with the Volume Purchase Program (VPP). You do not add these directly in the console. Instead, you set up a connector to VPP and they'll be synced in and ready for deployment.

- **Web link** – Deploy any website you can think of with a web link.

Windows 10 app types:

- **Microsoft Store app** – These are not very commonly deployed, and the end-user experience is not great. With store apps, you must first find the URL for the app (by searching the online app store) and paste it in the app creation process. These apps can only be deployed with the "Available" intent and when it comes to installing them users are redirected to the app within the Windows Store app.

- **Microsoft Store for Business (MSFB) app** – Comparable to Apple's VPP, MSFB apps are acquired in the Microsoft Store for Business (or Microsoft Store for Education) and automatically synced to Intune for deployment. There are a few advantages to deploying MSFB versions of applications instead of store versions; primarily the fact that these apps can be deployed as "Required" (so they install on PC's automatically without any user action).

- **Microsoft 365 Apps (Windows 10)** – Create a suite of Office apps, choosing from Access, Excel, OneDrive, Outlook, PowerPoint, Publisher, Skype for Business, Teams, Word or premium licensed apps like Project and Visio. The experience also lets you configure a bunch of customizations for the app package including the update channel and language packs.

- **Windows app (Win32)** – Win32 apps include both third-party and custom in-house developed applications. These apps will need some preparation before you can deploy them (you'll need to 'wrap' them into an .intunewin file format) with MEM but there are some significant advantages to doing so.

- **Microsoft Edge (Windows 10)** – The Microsoft first-class experience for deploying the Edge browser on Windows 10 managed devices. Under the covers, this is just another Win32 app deployment, but with a beautifully simple deployment experience.

- **Windows Line-of-Business (LOB) Apps** – These apps require an upload package. The uploaded package can be either a modern (.appx or .appxbundle) or legacy package (.msi) file format. You might choose to deploy .msi files in rare cases where the Win32 app type does not work for you.

- **Web link** – Type any valid URL and it will be deployed to managed Windows 10 PC's and arrive in the start menu.

Android

- **Managed Google Play Store app** – Browse and choose from apps in the Managed Google Play store and have them synced to the MEM console for deployment.

- **Managed Google Play private app** – The Managed Google Play store has an experience where you can upload your own .apk file. Once you do, you can make it available within your company's own private managed Play Store and sync it to MEM as a private app where it can be deployed.

- **Managed Google Play web link** – Enter any URL that should be deployed as a web link. You do this within the Managed Google Play store experience and have it synced to MEM for deployment.

- **Android Enterprise system app** – These "System" apps are apps that come already installed on devices but are hidden by default to end-users. Say you have a Samsung phone enrolled into Android Dedicated mode, end-users are not going to see any of the built-in Samsung apps that come preinstalled (like the photo gallery) so you first need to create the app as a system app. The process of creating a system app is straightforward, you just enter the publisher and package name.

- **Android Line-of-Business (LOB) app** – If you have an Android app file in .apk format then you'll upload it to MEM as a LOB app. This app type only works on the old, deprecated Android device administrator management mode.

- **Built-in Android app** – These are a curated list of Android store apps. The special thing about these apps is that they can be used with MEM's app protection policies.

- **Web link** – Type any valid URL and it will be deployed to managed Android devices. This app type is only for the old, deprecated Android device administrator management mode.

- **Android store app** – Again, this app type is out of fashion as Google discontinued support for Android device administrator management mode, but I'll list it here for completeness. You create an Android app by first finding the Google Play Store URL for an app and pasting it into the MEM console along with other app metadata.

- **Managed Android line-of-business app (deprecated)** – This app type is replaced by Built-in apps.

- **Managed Android store app (deprecated)** – This app type is replaced by Built-in apps.

Assigning apps to users and devices

Apps do not have any impact on your devices or users until you assign them. For assignment, you'll first need to create and populate the Azure AD user or device groups.

> **Tip! – Do you assign Apps to user or device groups?**
>
> There is no one-size-fits-all answer to this question but there are some basic rules and decision points.
>
> Do you want to deploy as Required or Available? If the latter, then you will need to use user groups.
>
> Other factors include app context and timing, particularly for Windows apps. The group type can determine if the app should be installed for one user or all Windows user profiles and whether the app can install while no users are logged on. To learn more, you can review this article: https://bit.ly/2RQD0oq.

Assignment type

Do you want to push the app down to enrolled devices or is this an optional app that you would rather users retrieve from a store themselves? Assignment type (also called *assignment intent)* is a term we use for this choice when it comes to deploying applications:

- **Required** – The app gets installed automatically, typically without any user interaction. This assignment type for apps can be used to "push" an app to a set of users or devices.

- **Available for enrolled devices** – The app gets published to the Intune Company Portal app (or the Managed Google Play store for Android work profile) and users can choose to install it from there themselves. This assignment type can only be used with user groups, not device groups.

- **Available with or without enrollment** – The app gets assigned to users and made available to install from the Company Portal. With this type, the devices do not need to be enrolled in MDM.

- **Uninstall** – The app gets uninstalled from devices that have installed it previously.

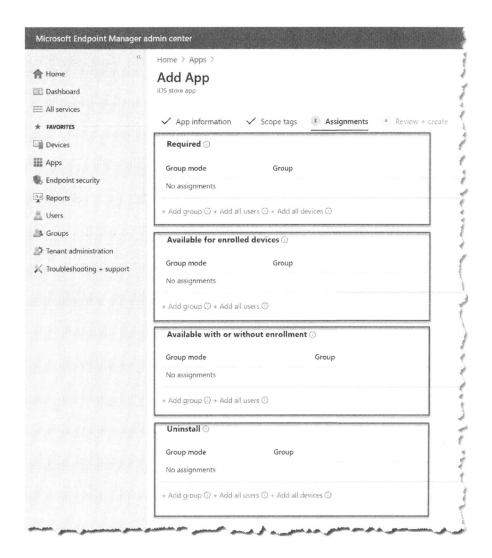

Group mode

The ability to "Exclude" a group from an assignment is a feature that exists for almost all workload assignments including Apps, Compliance and Configuration policies. The default mode for any app assignment is to *Include* a set of users or devices but with Group mode you could flip it to *Exclude* a set of users or devices. For example, you might have a large group, say "Australian users", that you use for assigning an app and later you find that there are 10 contractors in a group called "Contractors" that should not get the app due to regulatory requirements. Instead of having to create a third group "Australian users except contractors" you could use the *Exclude* group mode to ensure that just those 10 contractors don't get the app assignment.

> **Tip! – Don't mix User and Device groups with Group mode!**
>
> Mixing group types (User vs Device) with Group Mode (Include vs Exclude) is not supported. You can't assign to the "Finance Users" group and then create a "VIP devices" group for exclusion. Read the detailed Microsoft documentation on the scenario here: http://bit.ly/3i4k3uX.

Do it – Create and assign a required store app for iOS

In this exercise you will create and deploy an iOS store app to get familiar with the app creation flow. After completing these steps, I recommend branching out a bit further and trying out different app types available on the other platforms, too.

1. Sign in to the MEM admin center and go to *Apps > All Apps* then select *Add*.

2. Under *App type*, Select *iOS store app*.

3. On the *App information* page, select *Search the app store* and then search for any app you would find useful to deploy to users on iPhones or iPads (I usually search for "Microsoft" to get a list of all the Microsoft productivity apps).

4. Select one of the apps and the app information page will be populated with all the relevant app information.

5. Select *Next* and proceed to the *Assignments* page.

6. Under the *Required* section, select *Add group* and select one of the Azure AD user or device groups available for testing the deployment.

7. Complete the creation wizard and the store app will be deployed.

8. On an enrolled iOS device, test out the end-user experience. You will receive a notification to install the app. Note: this experience can be optimized so that there are no end-user prompts when using supervised devices and Apple VPP apps.

Do it – Create and assign a required Win32 app for Windows 10

In this exercise you will create and deploy a Windows 10 (Win32) app to get familiar with the creation flow. This app type can be somewhat complicated (due to the extra packaging steps needed) but provides a lot more flexibility than the other option of Windows line-of-business app type. The steps require you to download a special packaging tool from Microsoft and bundle the app into an *.intunewin* format that can be uploaded to MEM. After completing this exercise, I recommend branching out a bit further and trying some other (simpler) Windows app types, too!

1. Go to GitHub (www.github.com) and search for "Win32 content prep tool" (or use this direct short link: http://bit.ly/3oLjetk). You do not need to create a GitHub account.

2. Select *Code > Download ZIP* to begin downloading the tool to your management PC.

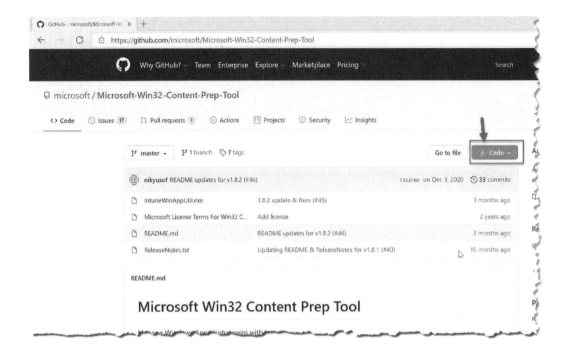

3. After the tool is downloaded, extract the contents from the zip. For my examples, I'm using the Windows default locations, so the tool is now located at *"C:\Users\<username>\Downloads\Microsoft-Win32-Content-Prep-Tool-master\Microsoft-Win32-Content-Prep-Tool-master\IntuneWinAppUtil.exe"*

4. Now find an app you want to package into MEM's .intunewin file format. If you don't have one in mind, download the popular Notepad++ application (https://notepad-plus-plus.org/downloads). Make sure you download the 64-bit installer in .exe format.

5. If necessary, create a new folder and copy the installer file(s) into it (this helps in the next step where the command line options require a directory as input.

6. Now open a new command prompt and change the directory to the location of the content creation tool. If using the defaults, the syntax would be as follows:

```
cd  c:\users\<username>\downloads\Microsoft-Win32-Content-Prep-Tool-mas-
ter\Microsoft-Win32-Content-Prep-Tool-master
```

7. Run the *IntuneWinAppUtil* tool from the command line.

```
IntuneWinAppUtil -c <setup_folder> -s <source_setup_file> -o <output_folder>
```

```
c:\Users\scottduf\Downloads\Microsoft-Win32-Content-Prep-Tool-master\Micros
oft-Win32-Content-Prep-Tool-master>IntuneWinAppUtil -c "c:\users\scottduf\D
ownloads\NotePadPlus" -s "c:\users\scottduf\downloads\NotePadPlus\npp.7.9.2
.Installer.x64.exe" -o "c:\users\scottduf\Downloads\NotePadPlus"
INFO    Validating parameters
INFO    Validated parameters within 12 milliseconds
INFO    Compressing the source folder 'c:\users\scottduf\Downloads\NotePadPl
us' to 'C:\Users\scottduf\AppData\Local\Temp\a9a574d6-5793-4a72-9b3e-71dbc3
bf70a5\IntuneWinPackage\Contents\IntunePackage.intunewin'
INFO    Calculated size for folder 'c:\users\scottduf\Downloads\NotePadPlus'
 is 4133472 within 3 milliseconds
INFO    Compressed folder 'c:\users\scottduf\Downloads\NotePadPlus' successf
ully within 287 milliseconds
INFO    Checking file type
INFO    Checked file type within 6 milliseconds
```

In this example I created a folder called NotepadPlus and used it as both the input and output folder.

8. Review the tool results and note the location of your new .intunewin file.

9. Now sign in to the MEM admin center and go to *Apps > All Apps* then select *Add*.

10. Under *App type*, Select *Windows app (Win32)*.

11. On the *App information* page, go to *Select app package file* and then upload the .intunewin file.

12. The app information page will be pre-populated with app information from the package. Update this information as required by adjusting the name, description, publisher or logo.

13. Select *Next* and proceed to the *Program* page.

14. To complete the *Program* page, you will need to know a little bit about the app – specifically, you need to know command-line options for installing and uninstalling, any return codes it uses to notify windows of progress and whether it requires a reboot. Often this information is available in vendor documentation, other times it may require some experimentation.

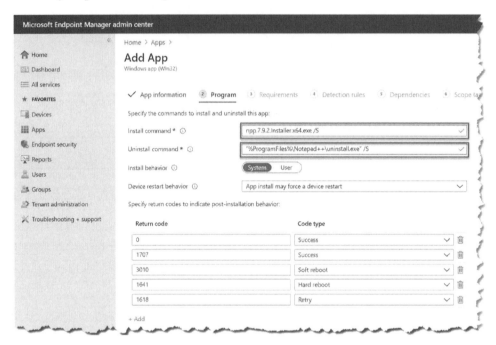

15. Proceed to the *Requirements* page. At a minimum, this page requires you to add a minimum supported Windows version and CPU architecture (32-bit or 64-bit). If you downloaded the 64-bit Notepad++ install file, choose 64-bit and select *Windows 10 1607*.

The requirements page also allows you to configure other advanced requirements such as the minimum number of CPU's or CPU speed. You can get even trickier by checking the presence of a registry key or a file on the hard disk. If you want to get super tricky with requirements you can use your own PowerShell script for detection.

16. Select *Next* to move to the *Detection rules page*. This page is where you tell MEM what it means when the app is installed and how it can detect the app.

17. For the Notepad++ example we will keep it simple and use the "File or folder" detection rule. Select *Manually configure detection* and add the required input details:

    a. Rule type: File

    b. Path: %ProgramFiles%\Notepad++

    c. File or folder: notepad++.exe

    d. Detection method: File or folder exists

18. Move to the *Dependencies* page and review the options available. If your software package requires other software to be installed first, then you can select it here. Since Notepad++ does not have any dependencies, select *Next*.

19. Continue the wizard to the *Assignments page*.

20. Under the *Required* section, select *Add group* and choose one of the Azure AD user or device groups available for testing the deployment.

21. Take note of the additional options for customizing the win32 app assignment. You can optionally configure Windows notification behavior for the app, delivery opti-

mization (when the app files will be installed) and the availability schedule (if you want the app to install straight away or after a deadline).

22. Complete the app creation wizard and the win32 app will be deployed to the group you specified.

23. Test whether the installation worked successfully on an enrolled Windows 10 device. Depending on the notification behavior you chose, you may notice some Windows 10 notifications appear and indicate progress.

Tip! – Trigger a sync!

If you don't see the app installation happening straight away you may need to sync the device, give it a reboot or just be patient. MEM must first install the *Intune management extension (IME)* on the device which is then used to install any subsequent win32 apps. You can check *services.msc* to see if the IME *s*ervice is installed to begin with, then dig deeper for app installation errors using device logs.

If the IME is installed but needs a kick to wake up and apply changes, Oliver Kieselbach gives a great tip on his blog (http://bit.ly/38eFG8a) – Just run this command to trigger a sync on-demand:

```
intunemanagementextension://syncapp
```

For a general view of installation results, you can review the *Device install status* report for the Win32 app in the MEM admin center. We will review other troubleshooting tips in Chapter 14.

Do it – Create and assign an Office App package for macOS

In this exercise you will walk through the simple creation experience for an Office 365 app deployment for macOS. A similar flow exists for Windows 10, too, except you have more options for selecting the apps in the suite and controlling update behavior. When you're done with macOS I recommend you walk through the Windows 10 experience, too.

1. Go to the MEM admin center and then to *Apps > All Apps* and select *Add*.

2. Under *App type*, Select *Microsoft 365 Apps for macOS*.

3. On the app information page, make any desired changes to name and description data and then select *Next*.

4. Complete the remaining app creation steps including assigning the app to a group as *Required*.

5. Test that the installation worked on an enrolled macOS device.

Managed app stores – VPP, MSFB and MGP

Apple has the Volume Purchase Program (VPP), Microsoft, the Microsoft Store for Business (MSFB) and Google, the Managed Google Play (MGP) store. These are all stores external from MEM where companies can acquire both paid and free apps to distribute via MDM. The basic flow for acquiring and distributing apps is this:

1. Create an account for your organization in the external third-party app store.

2. Browse a library of paid and free applications and pick some you want.

3. Link the external app store account to your MEM account.

4. Apps sync into MEM.

5. Assign the apps to groups of users or devices.

6. License usage (for paid apps) can be tracked by MEM.

When publishing an app to an app store, developers can choose to make their app available in these corporate app stores. They can make them generally available for any organization to purchase and distribute with MEM or they could publish a bespoke app to just one organization's account. Likewise, the app developer has control over other factors including availability in different geographical regions and pricing.

Apple Volume Purchase Program (VPP)

VPP allows you to get both free and paid apps for iOS/iPadOS and macOS devices in your environment. You can track license usage within the MEM console too.

VPP apps can provide a better end-user experience with fewer installation prompts than consumer store apps, but that depends on a couple of other factors. The most seamless user experience with zero prompts to install apps will require you to deploy these apps with device licensing on supervised devices. Read more about iOS prompts for VPP apps here: https://bit.ly/32SsFij.

Do it – Set up Apple VPP

1. Sign in to the MEM admin center, then navigate to *Tenant Administration > Connectors and Tokens > Apple VPP Tokens*.

2. Click *Create*.

3. On the *Basics* page, click on the link to *Open the Apple VPP Portal*. You will be directed to Apple Business Manager or Apple School Manager.

Note: Apple previously had separate admin portals for device enrollment programs and VPP management. The experience for both is now included in the Apple Business Manager (ABM) or Apple School Manager (ASM) portals, so depending on where your company is at in this migration, you might hit a web page asking you to choose which portal to use. We will only cover the newer (ABM/ASM) method in this book.

4. In the ABM portal, navigate to *Settings > Apps and Books*. Under *My Server Tokens*, next to the location select *Download*. You will see a .vpptoken file start downloading.

> Note: If there is no location listed you likely have not created any locations or the account you are signed in with does not have the Content Manager permission assigned for any location. You can resolve this by going to *Location* in the navigation menu, then finding your account in the *Accounts* section and adding the role.

5. Head back to the MEM admin center and the VPP Token create page.

6. Add a name for the connection, the Apple ID you used in the last step and upload the token you just downloaded from Apple.

7. On the settings page add a region and select *Business* or *Education*.

8. Tick the box to grant Microsoft permission to connect with Apple.

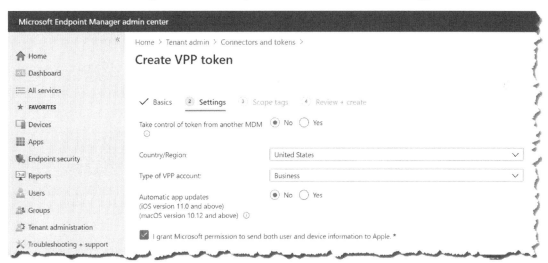

9. Complete the remaining VPP token creation steps and you will land on a page that shows the VPP connection as active.

10. Now return to the ABM or ASM portal to acquire apps.

11. Go to the *Apps and Books* page and start searching for apps you would like.

12. Once you find an app to acquire, specify the number of licenses and the location that you linked with the VPP token. These apps will start syncing to the MEM admin center *All apps* list and you can start assigning them as you would any other app.

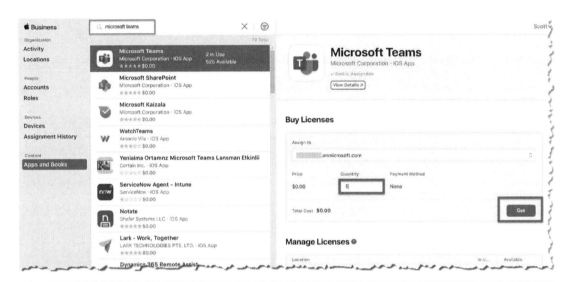

Tip! – Sync VPP Apps to MEM on demand

You can manually trigger a VPP connector sync from the MEM admin center by clicking on the '…' next to the token.

Microsoft Store for Business (MSFB)

The Microsoft version of VPP is the Microsoft Store for Business (MSFB) or Microsoft Store for Education (MSFE) when marketed to schools. There is a portal where admins can browse through listings of apps and then choose the ones they want. While there are some paid apps available, most apps acquired in MSFB are free, modern Windows 10 apps. Store apps will automatically update themselves to the latest version via built-in windows update channels. If you need to deploy modern Windows 10 applications to managed Windows 10 devices, it makes a lot of sense to set up the connection to MSFB and sync the apps for deployment. MSFB apps have some advantages over regular Microsoft store apps:

- MSFB apps can be deployed as "Required" but store apps can only be made "Available".

- MSFB apps can be configured to install in the device context, which means they can be installed once on the system, ready for all users, prior to any login.

- The process for browsing and adding apps for distribution is simpler and quicker than the Store app type.

The MSFB includes other capabilities that might be useful to your organization:

- **Choose between online and offline apps** – This feature allows you to download app installation packages (.appx and .appxbundle format) for offline deployment. MEM syncs both online and offline versions of applications once you set up the connector. The advantage of using offline licensed apps is that they can be deployed to device groups (instead of user groups) and installed before a user even signs in.

- **Line-of-business apps developer experience** – If you have contracted an app development team to create custom line-of-business applications then you can link the developer to your MSFB portal experience in a way that allows them to publish applications and updates directly into your tenant for distribution.

Do it – Set up MSFB

1. Sign in to the MEM admin center, then go to *Tenant administration > Connectors and tokens > Microsoft Store for Business*.

2. Follow the link to *Open the business store*. The business store web page will open in a new browser tab.

3. Sign in to the business store with your admin credentials. If this is the first time you are logging in there will be a short sign-up process to complete.

4. On the navigation menu, go to *Manage*, select *Distribution settings*.

5. Under *Management Tools*, select *Add management tool* and then select *Microsoft Intune*.

6. Now go to *Shop for my group*, and search for apps to deploy. Once you've found one you want to sync to MEM, select *Get the app*.

Tip! – Show offline licensed apps

Offline apps are hidden by default in the shopping experience. To start showing them, navigate to *Manage > Settings > Shop settings* and toggle the setting – *Show offline apps*: *Show offline licensed apps to people shopping in the Microsoft Store.*

7. Return to the MEM admin center MSFB connector setup page, choose a language (to control the language that apps are shown as in MEM) and select *Sync*.

8. MSFB apps will now start showing up in the MEM app list. Optionally, go to one of the apps and assign it to a group.

Managed Google Play (MGP)

Where the VPP and MSFB managed app stores and programs are optional, Android's Managed Google Play store setup is a key component of the Android Enterprise architecture and setting it up is a crucial step for any MEM admin.

Managed Google Play apps live in a web console (https://play.google.com/work). This is where you and other admins will acquire apps after connecting MGP to MEM. You can also create web apps and publish your own in-house developed Android apps for private distribution on this web page.

Tip! – Some Microsoft apps are added to MEM automatically

Some Microsoft apps are critical to MEM Android Enterprise scenarios and are automatically approved for you during the MGP connector setup process. You don't need to approve these manually. At the time of writing this book the apps are Microsoft Authenticator, Microsoft Intune, Intune Company Portal and Managed Home Screen.

Do it – Set up Managed Google Play

In Chapter 3 you set up the connection to the Managed Google Play store as a requirement for enrolling Android devices into Android Enterprise. If you skipped that chapter you should go back and set that up as a prerequisite for this exercise.

1. Go to the MEM admin center, then the Apps menu item.

2. Select *Add*, then select *Google Managed Play app*.

3. The managed Google Play store web page will open within the MEM console.

4. Browse the app listings and when you find one you want, choose *Approve*.

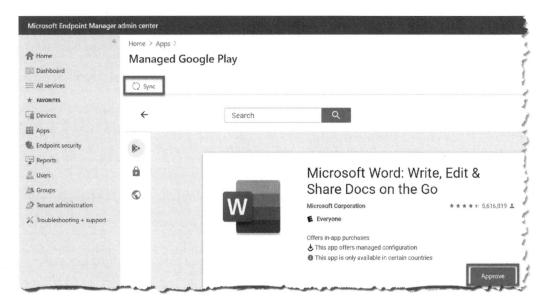

5. Review the permissions the app requires on the device then select *Approve*.

6. On the next page select *Keep approved when app requests new permissions*. This option prevents you from having to review and approve the application each time the developer updates it. If you don't do this, a developer update will pause all new installations and updates.

7. Select *Sync* and return to the apps list. The approved MGP apps will start showing up.

8. Optionally, assign these apps to groups to test the end-end experience.

End-user app stores for "Available" apps

The Company Portal is MEM's cross-platform, user-facing, self-service app. Its main purpose (besides enrollment) is to be the user's enterprise app store – a place where they go and see a curated list of apps available to install.

When you create an app in MEM and deploy it with one of the "Available" assignment types, the targeted users will be able to see the app listed in the Company Portal app. During the app creation process you will notice some of the fields that you edit are used to populate the Company Portal app listing. User-facing app information includes:

-   **Name** – A user-friendly app name that helps users identify the app at a glance.

-   **Description** – This description is usually pre-populated when the app was synced from another app store such as the MSFB, but you can edit and customize it for your organization. You can use markup (which is like a simpler version of HTML) to highlight things in this description. For example, you can add hyperlinks to further reading or bullet points when describing the installation or setup steps.

-   **Publisher** – This is usually pre-populated when syncing apps from other app stores, but you can edit it. Users will be able to see and filter app lists based on publisher.

-   **Category** – You are the boss of app categories. There are nine built-in ones like *Books and Reference* and *Productivity*, but you are free to create more categories and then organize apps into those categories to make it easier for users to find. For example, you might want to create categories for certain functions of your organization such as "IT Department Tools" or "Human Resources Apps".

-   **Featured** – If you toggle an app to be featured, it gets a prime position within the Company Portal experience. The position of featured apps varies based on the

Company Portal app platform, but in the case of Windows, featured apps appear first on the App home page.

- **Information URL** – This can be a "learn more" link. If there is a need to point users to an external link for further reading, support or instruction then you can use this app property.

- **Privacy URL** – Another "learn more" link where users can learn more about privacy in the app.

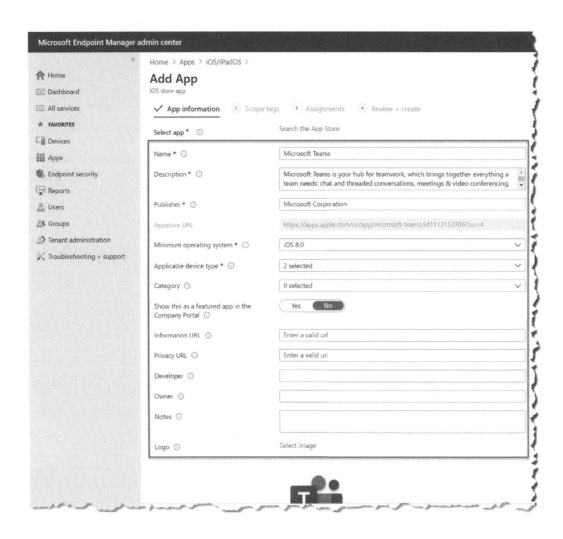

Distributing the Company Portal app to users

For users to see apps you make "Available", they will need to use the Company Portal. Users can install the Company Portal themselves from one of the consumer app stores, use the web version or have it magically appear on their device (because you cleverly deployed it as a required app on managed devices). Let's take a look at the different options available and how to get them.

Apple

The Company Portal is published in several places for use on Apple devices:

- **Apple App Store** – For iOS/iPadOS devices, users can download the app themselves. For any BYOD scenarios, this is the starting point for MEM enrollment so having it there to be used as an app store means no additional steps. To take care of those devices enrolled via a corporate enrollment method (like Apple's automated device enrollment program) you will want to add the Company Portal app to MEM via the *Add store app* experience and deploy it to a broad group with the *Required* assignment type. The apple store listing for the Company Portal is here: https://apps.apple.com/us/app/intune-company-portal/id719171358.

- **Direct download** – For macOS devices, there is no public macOS app store listing for the Company Portal app. If users don't already have the Company Portal app installed (if their device was enrolled via a corporate enrollment method) then you can instruct them to download it via a direct Microsoft download link: https://go.microsoft.com/fwlink/?linkid=853070.

Android

The app store experience for users on Android Enterprise enrolled devices is the Managed Google Play store, which is already installed on devices and does not require any additional

Company Portal app installation. The Company Portal app provides other functionality on Android Enterprise enrolled devices (e.g., Enrollment and User self-service of compliance) but it does not play a role in being an app store.

Even though the Company Portal app won't be the place your users go on Android Enterprise enrolled devices, they still might use it for apps in other scenarios. For example, you may choose to deploy apps "without enrollment" in which case users will still use the app. I'll further lay out all the places that Microsoft makes this app available to you and end-users.

- **Google Play Store** – To get BYOD Android devices enrolled for the first time your users will find the Company Portal app in the public Google Play store. The app listing can be found here: https://play.google.com/store/apps/details?id=com.microsoft.intune.

- **Managed Google Play store** – If your Android devices have been enrolled into the service without needing the Company Portal, you can push it as a required app post enrollment. You don't need to go add the app from the managed Google Play store though, the app is automatically acquired during Android Enterprise setup. The listing is here: https://play.google.com/work/apps/details?id=com.microsoft.windowsintune.companyportal.

- **China app stores** – Since the Google Play store isn't available to users In the People's Republic of China, Microsoft has published the Company Portal app into some of the other local app stores so users can retrieve it more easily. Search the Xiaomi, OPPO, Lenovo and Baidu app stores if your company operates in this region. More information on Microsoft docs: http://bit.ly/3dzu8j3.

- **Direct download** – For all other cases, Microsoft has published the Company Portal app package here to download and distribute as a LOB app: https://www.microsoft.com/en-us/download/details.aspx?id=49140.

Tip! – Don't confuse the *Company Portal* app with the *Microsoft Intune* app on Android

MEM develops two similar apps for Android, and they are both available in the public and managed play stores. The Company Portal app is used on Android Enterprise work profile scenarios and the Microsoft Intune app is used in the others. With Android Enterprise, neither of these apps act as an enterprise app store – users are directed to Managed Google Play store for that.

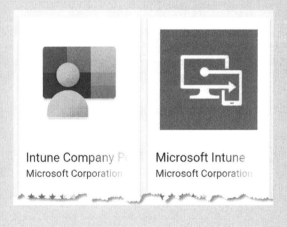

Windows 10

All available apps come from the Company Portal app on Windows 10 devices. The app can come from the following places:

- **Microsoft Store** – The Company Portal app is not needed for the enrollment of Windows devices but still plays a big role in being an app store. Users can search the Microsoft Store themselves to find it or use the direct link: https://www.microsoft.com/store/productId/9WZDNCRFJ3PZ.

- **Microsoft Store for Business** – In almost all scenarios, I'd recommend you acquire the Company Portal from the MSFB or MSFE. After setting up the connector between MEM and MSFB you'll just browse and acquire it, sync it to your tenant and then deploy it widely as a required app. In some offline scenarios where the MSFB is not available (for example, government clouds), you can download an offline app package which can then be uploaded to MEM as an LOB app. The MSFB Company Portal app listing can be found at this link:

https://businessstore.microsoft.com/store/details/company-portal/9WZDNCRFJ3PZ.

Web (across all platforms)

Users can browse available apps on any platform using the web version of the Company Portal.

- **Company Portal Web** – A good, lightweight, cross-platform alternative to deploying the available apps is to have users go to the web portal. It has a simple user interface that allows them to find and install apps without downloading the Company Portal App first. Users can access the Company Portal website by signing in with their Azure AD credentials, they don't need to be on an enrolled device. In fact, a good use of the web portal is to deploy LOB apps to unenrolled devices. Users can reach the web portal at this link: https://portal.manage.microsoft.com.

Tip! – Web portal vs fat App. Which one should I send my users to?

My advice is to deploy the fat version of the Company Portal app (as a required app) for each platform that you support. When devices are enrolled, they'll get it by default. The reason for this is that installed apps generally have better access to run code locally on your devices which usually equals a better user experience. For example, when you start installing an app within the Windows Company Portal app it begins monitoring the installation status so that it can notify the user as soon as the app finishes installing. On the other hand, the web portal doesn't have the same access to local devices and can't show app installation progress information.

180

CHAPTER 9

APP PROTECTION POLICIES

If your goal is to protect corporate data, but not enforce heavy-duty device controls, app protection policies (APP's) are for you. These security-style settings are applied to mobile apps without affecting device-level settings. For example, you can define a security PIN just for when users are logging into the Microsoft Outlook mobile app on their smart-phones – this is separate from the user's device PIN and only applies to the corporate data in the Outlook app.

App protection policies offer an easy, low friction way to enable BYOD. This is because devices do not actually need to be enrolled in MDM to receive policies and there is no special enrollment procedure for users to go through. Popular Microsoft apps (Outlook, Work, Excel, PowerPoint, Teams and others) are integrated with MEM's APP SDK which means that when a user signs in with a corporate account, they'll automatically pull down and apply user-assigned app protection policies.

Tip! – What is Mobile Application Management (MAM)?

When it first released, app protection policies (APP) were named mobile application management (MAM) policies. Later, Microsoft rebranded to APP to distinguish it from the already overloaded MAM term in the MDM industry that was used to describe a broad set of features around app management on mobile devices. Another abbreviation that you might see is "-WE", as in MAM-WE or APP-WE. The 'WE' stands for "Without Enrollment" and is referring specifically to policies that do not require enrollment in MDM.

Tip! – Platform support for APP

Android and iOS are supported platforms for APP policies. Windows 10 does have an equivalent feature called "Windows Information Protection (WIP)" but so many of the concepts and architecture are different that we will cover them separately in this chapter.

How do app protection policies work?

Microsoft builds and maintains an Intune APP software development kit (SDK) which is integrated into all Microsoft's popular mobile apps. The SDK does all the hard work when it comes to retrieving policies from MEM and applying them in the app. Here is the basic flow:

1. In MEM you configure the right set of security settings for your organization and define the apps and group of users that those settings will apply to.

2. Users get the app they need directly from an app store (for unmanaged devices) or you deploy it to them (for managed devices).

3. Users open the app and sign in. The app protection settings are automatically delivered and applied.

Tip! – Additional Android requirements for app protection policies

For Android, part of the magic is implemented within code in the Company Portal app. This means that the end-user experience for Android is a little different from iOS – users are prompted to install the Company Portal app when an app detects that APP settings need to be enforced.

App protection policy targeting options

App protection policies need to be assigned to user groups (Not device groups). You choose the Azure AD group of users or apply it to "All users" (which is a virtual group containing all licensed users). In real-world production deployments, you will likely end up with multiple groups of users who need different APP's targeted to them. Microsoft also has a set of recommendations for creating deployment rings for safe APP rollouts. Read more on that here: https://bit.ly/3nbKP6O.

The policy itself has options for more targeting granularity. You can define specific apps that should be protected with this policy and in some cases, you can target the policy only to specific devices (for example, only Android Enterprise enrolled devices).

Below are the device targeting options for APP:

iOS:

- All (default)
- Unmanaged
- Managed

Android

- All (default)
- Unmanaged
- Managed (Android Enterprise)
- Managed (Android Device Administrator)

Do it – Try out app protection policies

In this exercise you will create and deploy an app protection policy for iOS. When you are done, I recommend walking through the same steps for Android devices.

1. In the MEM admin center, go to *Apps > App protection policies*.

2. Select *Create policy*, then choose *iOS/iPadOS*.

3. Provide a name description for your policy (for example, iOS Policy for Outlook).

4. On the *Apps* page, leave the default targeting options – the policy will apply to devices in both managed and unmanaged states.

5. Navigate to *Select public apps* and view the list of apps that support app protection policies. Choose *Microsoft Outlook* from the list and then select *Next*.

6. On the *Data protection* page, choose the app protection settings you want to try. I recommend configuring the cut/copy/paste setting because it is an easy one to demo on test devices. The setting name is *Restrict cut, copy paste between other apps: Policy managed apps*. Select *Next*.

7. On the *Access requirements* page, customize any additional setting options. The defaults will enforce a 4-digit PIN for the Outlook app. Select *Next*.

8. On the *Conditional Launch* page review the options and make any additional customizations. These options can be used to define actions based on certain conditions. For example, if a user attempts to enter a PIN too many times while trying to access Outlook, you could choose to wipe all the corporate data from Outlook or just have them reauthenticate with credentials and then set a new pin. Select *Next*.

9. On the *Assignments* page, choose a user group to assign the policy.

Tip! – App protection policies are only supported to be assigned to user groups, not device groups.

10. Complete the wizard steps and then select *Create*.

11. On a freshly reset, unmanaged iOS device, go to the Apple App Store and install the *Microsoft Outlook* app.

12. Sign in to the app using a user account that is part of the user group to which you assigned the policy.

13. Once you sign in, the Outlook app will poll MEM and pull down any relevant app protection policies. You will know this has occurred because you will see the message *"Your organization is now protecting its data in this app. You need to restart the app to continue."* Select *Ok* and the app will close.

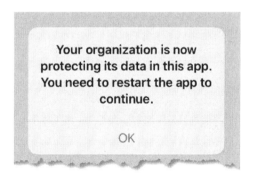

14. Open Outlook again and you will receive a new message – *"Your IT administrator is now helping you protect work or school data in this app."* Select ok.

15. You will now be prompted to set up a PIN for the Outlook app. Choose a PIN that complies with the complexity requirements that you defined in the policy.

16. Now in the Outlook app you can test whether your policy is working by attempting to copy and paste content from a protected app (an Outlook email) to an unprotect-

ed app (such as the notes app on iOS). Notice that the content is replaced by text: *"Your organization's data cannot be pasted here."*

17. As a bonus step, try out more app protection policy settings and test the resulting user experience. You will need to wait 30 minutes for the policy to refresh on the device.

Tip! – To avoid waiting for app protection policies to refresh you can sign out of the app and then sign in again. For apps that do not have a "sign-out", you can remove them and then re-install.

Supported apps and preparing your own

All the popular Microsoft apps have support for app protection policies and many third-party app developers are following suit by integrating Microsoft's SDK into their app or developing an Intune (MEM) specific version of their app. Below is a list of currently supported apps.

Microsoft apps:

- Field Service Mobile

- Microsoft Azure Information Protection Viewer

- Microsoft Bookings

- Microsoft Cortana

- Microsoft Dynamics CRM

- Microsoft Edge

- Microsoft Excel

- Power Automate

- Microsoft Kaizala

- Microsoft Launcher

- Microsoft Office

- Microsoft OneDrive

- Microsoft OneNote

- Microsoft Outlook

- Microsoft Planner

- Microsoft PowerApps

- Microsoft Power BI

- Microsoft PowerPoint

- Microsoft SharePoint

- Microsoft To Do

- Microsoft Skype for Business

- Microsoft StaffHub

- Microsoft Stream

- Microsoft Teams

- Microsoft Visio Viewer

- Microsoft Whiteboard

- Microsoft Word

- Microsoft Work Folders

- Yammer

Third-party apps:

- Acronis Access

- Adobe Acrobat Reader

- Blackberry Enterprise BRIDGE

- BlueJeans Video Conferencing

- Board Papers

- Breezy for Intune

- Box for EMM

- CellTrust SL2™ for Microsoft Intune

- Cisco Jabber for Intune

- Citrix Secure Mail

- Citrix ShareFile for Intune

- Egress Secure Mail for Intune

- Hearsay Relate for Intune

- iBabs for Intune

- ISEC7 MED for Intune

- Lexmark Mobile Print Intune

- Meetio Enterprise

- Nine Work for Intune

- Now® Mobile - Intune

- PrinterOn for Microsoft

- Qlik Sense Mobile

- SAP Fiori

- ServiceNow® Agent - Intune

- ServiceNow® Onboarding - Intune

- Smartcrypt for Intune

- Speaking Email

- Synergi Life

- Tableau Mobile for Intune

- Tact for Intune

- Vera for Intune

- Workspace ONE Send

- Zero for Intune

- Zoom for Intune

The list of supported apps is ever expanding, with new apps integrating the SDK regularly. I recommend checking the Microsoft docs page for the latest list of apps: https://bit.ly/347HA7z.

Preparing your own apps

Microsoft and third-party apps integrate the Intune APP SDK in order to leverage MEM's APP capabilities, but if your company has its own apps, there are a couple of ways to harness that power. There are two methods to enable LOB apps for app protection policies:

- Intune App Wrapping Tool

- Intune App SDK

There are a few considerations when choosing the best way to prepare your own apps, but generally the decision comes down to knowing who develops the LOB app. If your company has a team of developers who build and update line-of-business apps then your choice will likely be the SDK since it provides many more protection features and is easier to keep up to date over time and with each app version release. Conversely, if your company bought an app from an independent software developer (ISV) and you only have an .ipa (for iOS) or .apk file (for Android) with no access to source code or app update revisions then your only option might be wrapping it with the Intune App Wrapping Tool.

For the full list of features only available with the SDK I recommend looking at the feature table that is kept up to date in Microsoft docs: https://bit.ly/3l0aVaG.

Windows Information Protection (WIP) for Windows 10

App protection policies can be created for the Windows 10 platform in the MEM admin center, but it works very differently to everything I have described so far. The underlying technology powering data protection is a Windows 10 OS component called Windows Information Protection (WIP) rather than an Intune SDK.

WIP can be used in BYOD scenarios for Windows 10. The idea is that when users are working on their own Windows 10 devices, you can give them access to corporate data but keep it separate and encrypted from the personal content. Within a WIP policy, you start by defining a list of your corporate apps. Then you configure your corporate data locations, for example IP networks, or websites. Once you have created the policy and deployed it to users, they will have an experience where Windows 10 blocks certain actions – for example, users will be blocked from copying and pasting data from one of the corporate locations to a personal one. One of the better features of WIP is that any corporate data that users saved to their own hard drive was saved with WIP encryption. The data can be remotely removed by IT admins by revoking the encryption key if the user ever leaves the organization.

Tip! – Should I use Windows app protection policies?

The marketing slogan for WIP is "Keeping honest users honest". This tells you it is not a water-tight solution for Data Loss Protection (DLP) on Windows 10. The solution was built to prevent accidental data leakage but not to combat malicious users or hackers. There are known tricks for users to circumvent the protections and your IT security team will probably poke holes in this as a viable solution quickly. It's also very hard to configure broad enterprise-ready policies properly – you'll need to go through a lengthy auditing-only mode process to identify all the corporate apps and locations, then another lengthy data collection phase where the policy is turned on in audit only mode.

My advice is that this feature can be a useful tool that makes up a multi-layered Windows 10 DLP strategy, but do not count on it as your one and only data protection solution for Windows 10 BYOD.

CHAPTER 10

APP CONFIGURATION POLICIES

App configuration is a neat little feature that allows you to configure app settings. Imagine a scenario where you found a cool app for employees to use but it needs some company-specific setup such as a company-specific code, URL, IP address or port number to get it working. This is where app configuration shines!

There are two types of app configuration policies available in MEM:

- Managed devices

- Managed apps

App configuration policies for managed devices

This mode of configuring apps only works on MDM-enrolled devices. The app itself needs to be developed in such a way that supports managed app configuration.

As an IT pro, you will first need to find out if the app you're deploying supports it. A good starting point is the developer's website support page. App configurations are defined in key-value pairs for iOS devices or XML for Android. The format also allows for variables or tokens in place of values. For example, {{userprincipalname}} could represent scott@endpointmanager.com. A good example of app config in action is in Microsoft's own mobile productivity apps (Word, Excel, PowerPoint, Outlook, Teams, Edge and a few others). These apps all include support for the setting "IntuneMAMAllowedAccountsOnly" which configures the app to only allow a single, corporate identity sign-in and block personal accounts. Other Microsoft apps such as the Microsoft Launcher/Managed Home Screen (for Android) app or MEM's own Company Portal app support managed device app configuration settings and a few third-party enterprise apps have support too:

- Chrome browser (Android) – https://bit.ly/3nPOc3G

- SAP JAM (iOS and Android) – https://bit.ly/3lLYX4W

- Acrobat (iOS and Android) – https://adobe.ly/3nS4l8s

- Zoom (iOS and Android) – https://bit.ly/3drDlIr, https://bit.ly/315iTYK

- Slack (iOS and Android) – https://bit.ly/34PDaCw

- Dropbox (iOS and Android) – https://bit.ly/3nS8ut2

Tip! – Enabling app config in your own LOB Apps

Developing your own line-of-business apps with app configuration is outside the scope of this book but if this is something you're interested in, you can take a look at the iOS and Android documentation and samples:

Android managed configurations – https://bit.ly/318PXPI

iOS managed app configuration – https://apple.co/34THr8h

One other great resource is the AppConfig community website found at https://www.appconfig.org. The AppConfig community is a collection of UEM companies (Microsoft is not one of them) and developers that team up to standardize mobile app config.

Do it – Try out app configuration policies for managed devices

In this exercise you will create an Android app config policy for Google Chrome and assign it to a user group. You will use a basic app configuration setting to set the Google Chrome homepage, but I also recommend exploring and experimenting with other available settings.

1. Go to the MEM admin center, then go to *Apps > App configuration policies*.

2. Select *Add*, then choose *Managed devices*.

3. Add a name for the policy. For example, "Google Chrome corporate bookmarks on Android".

4. Select *Android Enterprise* as the platform and *Personally-owned work profile only* as the *Type*.

5. In the *Select app* context menu, search for and select *Google Chrome*. If Chrome does not show up in the app list, you will need to add it to MEM first. Go back to *Apps > All apps > Add > Managed Google Play app* and search for it in the Google Play Store, then approve it so it syncs to MEM. Assign it to the same group where you plan to assign the App configuration policy.

6. Select *Next*.

7. On the settings page you have the option to define the configurations with the configuration designer or copy/paste JSON formatted text. Choose *Use configuration designer* then select *Add*.

8. In the open context pane, browse the list of settings available for Chrome and then locate the setting *Managed bookmarks*. Select it and then *Okay*.

9. In the *Configuration value* field enter a test URL (Example: https://endpoint.microsoft.com).

10. Complete the creation wizard and assign the policy to the same user group where you assigned the Chrome app.

11. Use an existing enrolled device (or enroll a new Android test device by downloading the Company Portal app and walking through the enrollment flow for the Android Enterprise work profile). The test user account you use for enrollment should be a member of the group that you assigned the app and app config policy to.

> **Tip!** – To help troubleshoot settings applied in Chrome, you can type *about:policy* in the Chrome browser address box. Chrome will display all the app config values that were applied by MEM.

App configuration policies for managed apps

Using the *Managed apps* policy type has a huge advantage over *managed devices* because it works without requiring MDM enrollment. In this mode of app configuration, the Intune app SDK is embedded inside applications and brokers configuration over the same channel used for app protection policies. The only downside is that not all third-party apps have integrated Intune's app SDK to support it. When users sign in to SDK-enabled mobile apps with their corporate identity, the SDK reaches out to MEM and pulls down settings that you defined as key/value pairs in the MEM admin center. The SDK then hands those over to the app, which understands exactly how to apply those settings in the app.

These Microsoft apps support app configuration without enrollment:

- **Microsoft Edge browser** – Define bookmarks, branding, extensions and security settings on iOS and Android (https://bit.ly/2STAtui).

- **Office Mobile** (combines Word, Excel, PowerPoint) – Define sticky note behavior and sharing settings on iOS and Android (https://bit.ly/3jYh86V).

- **Outlook mobile** – Many settings including disabling Focused Inbox (my favorite), Calendar and contact sync and notifications (https://bit.ly/315UClw).

Do it – Try out app configuration policies for managed apps

In this exercise you will create an app configuration policy for managed apps. We will create a simple configuration that turns off my personal least favorite feature of the Outlook mobile app – the Focused Inbox. While there is a first-class MEM admin center experience for deploying first-party app config for Outlook, you should note that the underlying feature allows you to push down many more settings by defining key:value pairs. That means you can easily apply custom settings defined by other third-party developers in the other apps that your company uses.

1. Go to the MEM admin center, then *Apps > App configuration policies*.

2. Select *Create*, then select *Managed app*.

3. On the *Basics* page, type a name and description for the policy. For example: "Turn off Outlook Focused Inbox".

4. Go to *Select public apps* and choose both Outlook for iOS and Android from the menu.

5. Select *Next*.

6. On the *Settings* page, under *Outlook configuration settings*, toggle *Focused Inbox* to *No*.

7. Assign the policy to a test user group and complete the policy creation wizard.

8. On an unmanaged device, download the *Microsoft Outlook* app from the app store and sign in with test user credentials. The settings will be applied silently.

9. Go to *Settings* in the Outlook app. You will notice the Focused Inbox setting is turned off and disabled.

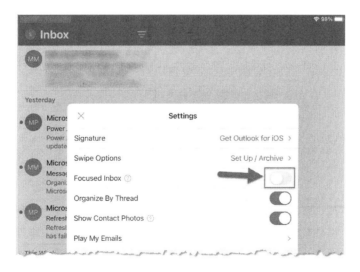

Guided scenarios and Policy sets

Now that you have learned about each of the different MEM workload types (Compliance, Configuration, Apps, app protection and configuration policies) I'll tell you about a shortcut that can create them all in one go and save you some time.

Guided scenarios simplifies the creation experience for all the workloads needed to make up a given scenario. For example, a guided scenario for *Deploy Microsoft Edge mobile* will create the app and MAM policies and have them assigned to the group of your choosing in a fast and friendly wizard. At the time of writing this book there are three scenarios: "Deploy Microsoft Edge for mobile", "Try out a cloud-managed PC" and "Secure Microsoft Office for mobile". Under the hood, the wizard will create a *Policy set*.

Policy sets are buckets of resources (apps, policies and other workloads) that you can group together and assign as a single entity. Instead of creating and assigning individual workloads to make up a device's configuration, *Policy sets* lets you group together all the workloads and assign them to a group in one hit.

As a bonus exercise, I recommend walking through the creation experience for both. You will find *Guided scenarios* on the *Home* navigation page for MEM, and *Policy sets* under *Devices > Policy sets*.

CHAPTER 11

CONDITIONAL ACCESS

Conditional Access (CA) lets you improve security in a cloud-first and mobile world. With companies moving their digital workplaces from secure on-prem perimeter networks to the cloud they are increasingly relying upon cloud-based apps, services and subscriptions. The traditional perimeter network security approach of blocking off network ports doesn't work anymore. CA is an engine that helps you adapt your security approach. It can help you ensure that when users access corporate data, they are who they claim to be and are accessing that data on a properly secured and compliant device, on a supported and secure app, from a known location or region.

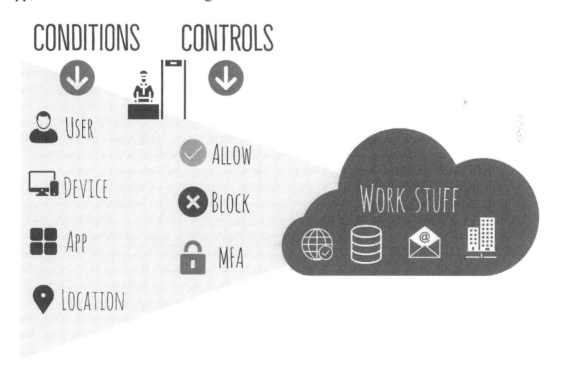

Building a CA policy in MEM is like hiring a new security guard to sit at the front door of your physical office and monitor the CCTV. You train the security guard by telling them about the conditions – which buildings to monitor, who to watch and what sort of suspicious behavior to look for. Lastly, you train the security guard on the controls. What should they do when someone tries to enter the building? Should she block them, let them in or ask them for more proof of identity such as an ID card?

In the same way, you "train" your CA engine by defining the conditions as user groups, cloud apps or other things about sign-in such as the client app or IP address they are coming from. Finally, you decide on what controls to implement – should you allow/ block access or require more security such as multi-factor authentication or force enrollment into MEM?

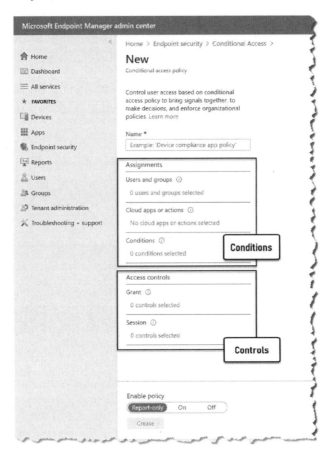

As a MEM admin, there are three settings in the **Controls** section of a CA policy that you should become familiar with:

- Grant access: Require device to be marked as compliant

- Grant access: Require approved client app

- Grant access: Require app protection policy

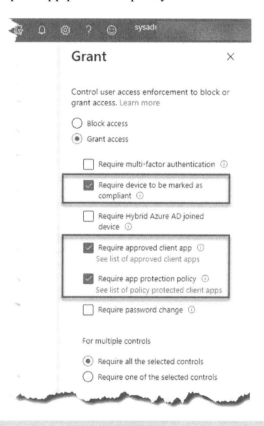

Tip! – Conditional Access can be accessed and configured in the MEM admin center under *Endpoint Security > Conditional Access* but this is just a shortcut for the convenience of MEM and endpoint security admins. CA is an Azure AD Premium feature (which is included in the EMS and Microsoft 365 subscriptions I recommended earlier in this book.

Device CA – Require compliant devices

Device CA is a security approach where you specify that a device must be marked as "Compliant" before being allowed to access corporate resources from it. For a device to be marked "Compliant" it needs to be enrolled in MDM and be targeted with a MEM compliance policy. Once that device has checked in with MEM and received the policy, MEM will evaluate it against all the settings in that policy and update the compliance status to either Compliant or Not compliant based on the result.

You can see if a device is compliant or not compliant by viewing the device object in both the MEM Admin Center and the Azure AD Portal. You can also view the compliance status on the corresponding device object in Azure AD.

APP-CA and MAM-CA – Require approved apps and app protection policy

The controls *Require approved client app* and *Require app protection policy* are often referred to as APP-CA and MAM-CA. These controls help you strengthen your security posture without burdening users by forcing them down the MDM enrollment path. It is worth pointing out at this point that both controls are only for mobile apps and do not apply to Windows 10 or macOS.

Require approved client app

The effect of ticking this box is that targeted users can access corporate resources but only from a Microsoft pre-defined and hard-coded list of mobile applications. For example, users can only access their Office 365 email using the Outlook mobile app. They would be blocked from using native email apps or any other third-party mail clients. The security promise is that this pre-defined list of apps supports MEM app protection policies (APP). With APP-CA you can force users to leverage only securable apps to access corporate data. The gap is that the apps, although they support app protection policies, do not necessarily need to have one applied – that's where MAM-CA comes in.

> **Tip! – Which apps support the APP-CA control?**
>
> Most of the Microsoft productivity apps for mobile include the Intune APP SDK and therefore are in the hard-coded list of approved apps. This changes frequently though, so I recommended checking the latest list: https://bit.ly/3k04fcG.

Require app protection policy

This setting is an enhancement to app-based Conditional Access controls. While the "Require approved client app" control ensures users are signed in with an approved app, it does not strictly check that the device received the app protection policy and successfully applied all the security settings. This setting addresses that gap by ensuring app protection policies are applied before the user can use the app to access corporate data.

CA user experiences and broker apps

For Azure AD to securely determine if a device is enrolled, compliant, using an approved app or using an approved app *with an app protection policy*, there is a requirement that the device be "Azure AD Registered" (also known as workplace joined).

Device registration into Azure AD is a lightweight process that creates a device record in Azure AD that the Conditional Access engine can refer to later. The way registrations happen on mobile devices is via a "broker app". There are two Microsoft broker apps – the MEM Company Portal app and the Microsoft Authenticator app. Windows 10 does not need a broker app because device registration is built into the operating system. On Windows 10, device registration can be observed by signing into any Microsoft modern UWP apps (for example, Microsoft OneNote) or manually from Windows under *Settings*, *Add work or school account*.

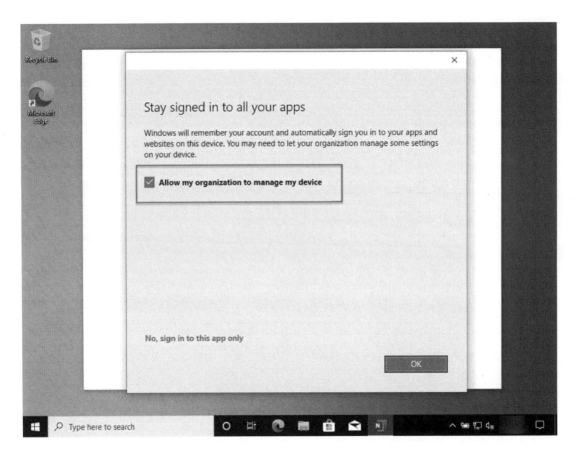

On iOS/iPadOS, the Company Portal or the Microsoft Authenticator app can function as a broker app, but on Android devices it must be the Company Portal. If users are targeted by an APP-CA policy and are on a device not Azure AD registered, they will first be redirected to the app store to install one.

Do it – Try out device CA

In this exercise you will walk through the creation of two CA policies for protecting access to Office 365. First, a device-based Conditional Access policy will force all desktop clients (Windows 10 and macOS) to be enrolled and compliant with MEM compliance policies. Second, a CA policy will apply to mobile devices and require the use of app protection policies.

- Part 1 – Create a device CA policy.

- Part 2 – Create an APP-CA policy.

- Part 3 – Test access to Office 365 from a Windows PC or macOS device.

- Part 4 – Test access to Office 365 from mobile devices.

Part 1 – Create a device CA policy

1. Sign in to the MEM admin center and go to *Endpoint security > Conditional Access*.

2. Select *Create*.

3. Provide a name for the Device-CA Policy (Example: Require Compliant PC's for Office 365).

4. Under *Assignments*, in the *Users and groups* section, use the *Select users and groups* radio button to choose a test user group or specific test account.

5. In the *Cloud apps or actions* section, use the *Select apps* radio button and choose *Office 365* from the list of cloud applications.

6. In the *Conditions* section, select *Device platforms*, toggle it to *Configured* and select *Windows and macOS*.

7. Under the *Access controls* section under *Grant*, select the options to *Grant access - Require device to be marked as compliant*.

8. Finally, toggle the policy to *Enabled* and save it.

Part 2 – Create an APP-CA policy

9. On the Conditional Access landing page, select *Create*.

10. Provide a name for the APP-CA Policy (Example: Require app protection for Mobile devices).

11. Under *Assignments*, in the *Users and groups* section, use the *Select users and groups* radio button to choose a test user group or specific test account. This can be the same user you targeted with the first policy.

12. In the *Cloud apps or actions* section, use the *Select apps* radio button and choose *Office 365* from the list of cloud applications.

13. In the *Conditions* section, select *Device platforms*, toggle it to *Configured* and select *Android*, and *iOS*.

14. Under the *Access control* section under *Grant*, select both options *Grant access - Require approved client app* and *Require app protection policy*.

15. Select *Require all the selected controls*.

16. Now toggle the policy to *Enabled* and save it.

Part 3 – Test access to Office 365 from a Windows PC or macOS device

To test the first device-based CA policy, you should log onto a fresh (not MDM enrolled) Windows 10 PC or macOS device. If you don't have one available you could use your admin PC – just be sure to open a new *InPrivate* browser tab so no cached tokens from your admin get in the way.

17. Go to https://www.office.com and select *Sign in*.

18. Attempt to sign in with your test user Azure AD credentials. You should be blocked with a company-branded message: *You can't get there from here*.

You can't get there from here

This application contains sensitive information and can only be accessed from:

- Devices or client applications that meet Company name management compliance policy.

You need to be signed in to Microsoft Edge with the work or school account shown above. To sign in, click on your account image. Learn More

Sign out and sign in with a different account

More details

The CA policy we created applies to all client apps and browser sessions – this means the same blocking experience exists if you attempted the above access from the Outlook desktop app when attempting mailbox setup and sign-in.

19. Now enroll the device or attempt to access Office 365 from a different enrolled device – you will notice that you have uninterrupted access to office 365 from the browser or desktop client apps.

Part 4 – Test access to Office 365 from mobile devices

To test the APP-CA and MAM-CA policies you should log onto a fresh (unenrolled) iOS or Android mobile device. The steps below are for iOS but the Android experience is very similar – I recommend trying both.

20. On an unenrolled iOS device, open the default mail app and begin setting it up. On the *Welcome to mail* screen, choose *Microsoft Exchange* and then add the test user's email address, select *Next* and then *Sign in*.

21. You will be redirected to a company-branded Azure AD sign-in page. Enter the username and password for the test user.

22. Upon successful authentication, you will see an Azure AD block message: *You can't get there from here*.

23. Now attempt to connect to work email using the Outlook app. Download the Outlook app from the App Store and then sign in with the test user's Azure AD credentials.

24. After authenticating you will be prompted with an Azure AD message: *Help us keep your device secure*.

Help us keep your device secure

To continue, you must install the Microsoft Authenticator app and register your device. It helps keep organizational data more secure. More details

Get the app

25. Select *Get the app* and you will be redirected to the App Store to download *Authenticator* (if you are testing on an Android device you will be redirected to download the Company Portal app).

26. When the Authenticator app installs and opens, enter the test user credentials and then select *Register*.

Help us keep your device secure

Register your device to continue. More details

Register

27. After you register the device, you will be redirected to the Outlook app where setup will complete.

28. Before an email is displayed, the app protection policy message will appear – "Your organization is now protecting its data in this app. You need to restart to continue".

29. Open the Outlook app again and you will be able to see email and be protected by the app protection policies.

Session-based controls for CA

Device-CA and APP-CA are great controls, but you might still have some gaps that you want to fill. What about personal Windows devices? Do you want to allow workers to access corporate content at home on their PC and if so, do you really want them to enroll those PC's into MEM? A more common approach to this problem is to implement the Conditional Access session-based controls setting: *Use app enforced restrictions*.

App enforced restrictions can be created for SharePoint Online and Exchange Online cloud apps to provide users with restricted access when they are visiting from unmanaged devices such as home PC's. Conditional Access ensures that users can only reach SharePoint or Exchange from a web browser and when they access it, they are prevented from downloading any content to unprotected locations such as a local disk or external drive.

Do it – Try out session controls for CA

In this exercise you walk through the creation of session-based access controls for SharePoint Online. You will do this from the SharePoint Online admin website and then see that under the hood a new CA policy was created in Azure AD.

Create app-enforced CA policies in the SharePoint admin center

1. Go to the SharePoint admin website (https://admin.microsoft.com/sharepoint) and sign in with your admin credentials.

2. On the left navigation menu, go to *Policies > Access control*.

3. Select *Unmanaged devices: Restrict access from devices that aren't compliant or joined to a domain.* A new context pane will open with options for how to treat unmanaged devices.

4. Select *Allow limited, web-only access* and then save.

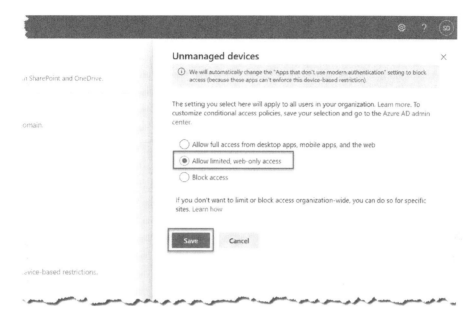

5. In a new tab, open the Conditional Access policy page by going to the MEM admin center > *Endpoint security* > *Conditional Access*.

6. Notice that there were two new policies created:

   a. *[SharePoint admin center]Block access from apps on unmanaged devices*

   b. *[SharePoint admin center]Use app-enforced Restrictions for browser access*

7. Open each of the policies and look at the pre-defined configurations – notice the user scope is set to "All users". You may change this scope to only your test user or group.

Test out the app-enforced policy for SharePoint Online.

1. On an unmanaged device, open a new InPrivate browser window.

2. Go to SharePoint Online (www.sharepoint.com) and sign in with the test user account.

3. Open an existing document from SharePoint or create a new one. You will notice the warning banner: *Your organization doesn't allow you to download, print or sync using this device. To use these actions, use a device that's joined to a domain. For help, contact your IT department.*

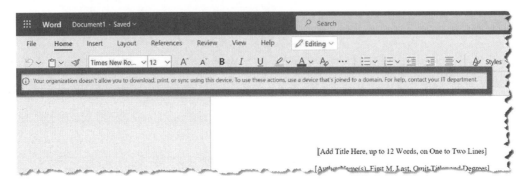

CHAPTER 12

CONFIGURATION MANAGER, CO-MANAGEMENT AND TENANT ATTACH

At the Microsoft Ignite conference in 2018, Brad Anderson – the CVP of Microsoft Commercial Management Experiences – announced the rebranding of Microsoft Intune and System Center Configuration Manager to one product: Microsoft Endpoint Manager (MEM). Since then, we have seen gradual innovation on cloud-powered features and the merging of experiences across the management boundaries. The product lines are fuzzy when it comes to which service components (Intune cloud or ConfigMgr server) are performing management at any one time. Rather than forcing customers to lift and shift Windows devices from on-prem to cloud management (which could mean large and lengthy projects for IT professionals), Microsoft instead implemented MEM features in a low-friction way where you attach your existing ConfigMgr environment (and managed devices) to the cloud. Once attached to the cloud, organizations can start to benefit from the new cloud features and innovation. In this chapter we will explore each of the management modes available for Windows 10 devices.

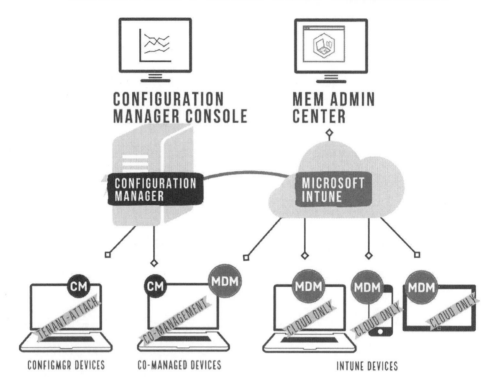

Configuration Manager device management in the MEM admin center

The MEM admin center represents the three states that a device can be in via the "managed by" label. The three states are:

- ConfigMgr (tenant-attached) devices

- Co-managed devices

- Intune devices

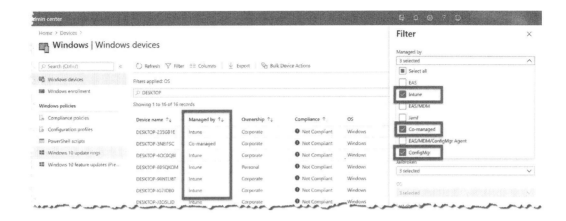

ConfigMgr devices (tenant-attached devices)

Tenant-attached devices have the Configuration Manager agent installed on them and they connect directly to your on-prem servers for management. They show up in the MEM admin center along with the Intune and co-managed devices so that you can have one cloud administration console for management even though Configuration Manager infrastructure is the sole entity delivering payload to devices. Just because these devices are tethered to on-prem ConfigMgr servers doesn't mean they need to stay inside the corporate network to be managed, though. They can stay in touch with ConfigMgr servers as long as they can reach the internet thanks to a Configuration Manager feature called a Cloud Management Gateway.

Co-managed devices

Co-managed devices have the Configuration Manager agent installed on them and are also enrolled in Intune via the Windows 10 MDM stack. Settings and applications can be delivered via Intune and Configuration Manager at the same time. To make sure both management entities don't step on each other's toes, you can choose which entity should be responsible at a workload level. For example, you can tell Intune to deliver compliance policies but keep ConfigMgr delivering the applications. There are two key paths to co-managing devices: you can either automatically enroll existing on-prem devices or you can add new devices directly into the cloud using Autopilot and other modern provisioning methods and then install the Configuration Manager agent as a final step to enable co-management.

Intune devices

Intune-only devices have cut the cord to on-prem management. They do not have any ConfigMgr agent installed on them, they are enrolled only in MDM and get policy only from Intune.

Tip! – MEM "Managed by" vs Azure AD "Join type"

I want to clear up any confusion you might have at this point about MEM's management type and the Azure AD join type. Just because a device is co-managed in MEM does not mean it is also Hybrid Azure AD joined (HAADJ). This table shows the valid combinations of Azure AD trust type and MEM management.

		Azure AD Join Type		
		AD Joined	AADJ Hybrid Join	AADJ only
MEM Management State	ConfigMgr	Yes	Yes	Yes
	Co-managed	No	Yes	Yes
	Intune	No	Yes	Yes

If your company is on a journey to the cloud with goals to eliminate all on-prem infrastructure (including Active Directory and domain controllers) then you shoot for the bottom-right option.

Co-management or Cloud-only? Choose the right strategy for your company

The management strategy for Windows devices at your company will come down to several factors. Before deciding on one of the three management modes for devices you should consider these questions:

- What management capabilities do we really need and are they available with cloud only?

- Are our Windows devices managed with Configuration Manager or another management product?

- Do we still need to manage down-level devices such as Windows 7?

- Do we have devices or segments of our network that are not connected to the internet?

- Does our company have goals to reduce or completely remove on-prem server footprint?

- Are we ready to embark on an app migration project to move Windows apps to the cloud?

- Is the team that manages or provides helpdesk support for mobile devices also the team that manages Windows 10 PC's?

After thinking about these questions, you might start to realize that there is no single approach. If your company is brand new, being born in the cloud, then the answer is easy but for most readers, your company will be carrying management baggage and accumulated technical debt. This is why MEM provides you with flexible options and progressions of cloud-value so that you can start getting benefits of cloud management straight away with minimal effort.

Here is the value you can expect at each progression:

1. Cloud-attach your existing ConfigMgr devices by deploying a Cloud Management Gateway (CMG). As soon as you do this they can be managed over the internet. The device management admin experience will remain in the on-prem Configuration Manager console at this step.

2. Tenant attach Configuration Manager servers to Intune. Now your helpdesk can use a single cloud admin console for Windows 10 device management. The actual management messages are still delivered from your own Configuration Manager server infrastructure.

3. Turn on co-management. Now you can deliver new cloud-only capabilities such as new types of configuration and compliance policies, Conditional Access and analytics without giving up any of the features you love (such as app management capabilities) from Configuration Manager.

4. Go cloud only. At this point you no longer need to host or manage Configuration Manager server infrastructure. All management payloads are configured in the MEM admin center and delivered from the cloud.

Tip! – A win for management over the internet

When the COVID-19 pandemic broke out in 2020, IT admins around the world scrambled to adjust their management capabilities so that they could support users working at home. A lot of customers relied on intranet-only connections between Configuration Manager and Client PC's but the IT admins who had already added Cloud Management Gateways were very happy with themselves – they didn't need to scramble, they had everything ready to support users over the internet.

Do it – Try out tenant attach

In this first exercise you will attach ConfigMgr infrastructure to Intune so that admins can begin to use the MEM admin center to manage on-prem Windows devices. The below steps assume you built a ConfigMgr lab environment based on the Azure template (Option 1 below), but the steps can be easily adapted to suit your own lab environment if you have one.

Options for setting up your ConfigMgr lab environment.

Option 1 (recommended) – Build one in Azure. This is a fast way to get all the server infrastructure built and ready to start these exercises. You can use an Azure ARM template to automate the entire process. The only downside is that you need to have an Azure subscription and pay for the servers you use. The cost for the four VM's and the storage account in the lab will be about USD 112 per month but you can keep costs way lower than that if you shut down the VM's when you don't need them. Another tip is to buy a Visual Studio subscription which gives you either $50, $100 or $150 per month credits to use in Azure – plenty enough to build a lab and get through these exercises.

The step-by-step instructions for setting up a ConfigMgr lab in Azure are documented in Microsoft docs: http://bit.ly/3a5bM6s

Option 2 – Build a lab using a hypervisor. You can build your own lab with VM's running on Hyper-V or other virtualization software. This is a good option if you don't have an Azure subscription with credits to spend on VM's. The downside is that building it is going to be less automated and take you a lot longer. Just follow the Microsoft documentation for setting up the lab from Microsoft docs: http://bit.ly/36jI2Sd

1. Connect to *CMlabPS01* and open the Configuration Manager console from the Start menu (Search for it or find it under the *Microsoft Endpoint Manager* folder).

2. Go to *Administration > Cloud Services > Co-management*.

3. Select *Configure Co-management*.

4. On the *Tenant onboarding* page, sign in with your administrator's credentials, keep the default selection of Azure environment as *AzurePublicCloud* and ensure *Upload to Microsoft Endpoint Manager admin center* is checked.

5. Uncheck the option *Enable automatic client enrollment for co-management*. We will enable co-management of devices in a subsequent exercise.

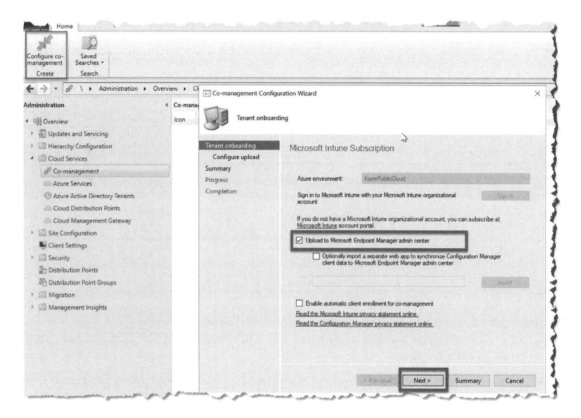

6. Select *Next* and accept the confirmation message to confirm you want to create an Azure AD application and authorize synchronization.

7. On the *Configure upload* page, accept the default option to upload all devices. It is not necessary to check the box to enable *Endpoint Analytics* for this exercise.

8. Select *Next* and then review and complete the wizard.

9. Now sign in to the MEM admin center and check that the connector has been add-

ed. Go to *Tenant administration > Connectors and tokens > Microsoft Endpoint Configuration Manager* and you will see the new server connection listed along with the last sync time.

10. Now go to *Devices > All devices > Windows devices*.

11. Notice that the on-prem Windows 10 devices are now showing in the MEM device list with a *Managed by* tag of "ConfigMgr".

12. Open one of the devices and explore the additional options that are available to initiate from the MEM admin center.

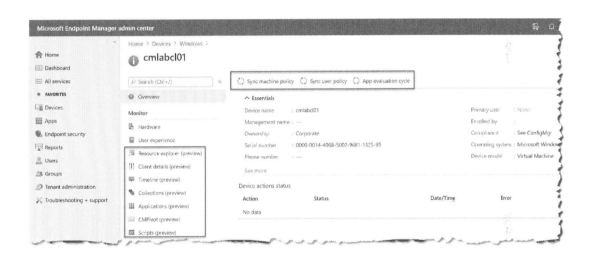

Do it – Enable Hybrid Azure AD Join for on-prem Active Directory devices

In this exercise you will get your environment ready for co-management by connecting your active directory domain to Azure AD. You will install a tool called Azure AD Connect which will start synchronizing users and groups from on-prem AD into Azure AD. More importantly, the tool will enable configure Hybrid Azure AD Join for your environment. The steps below assume you went with lab option 1 but you can adjust the steps to suit your own lab environment.

1. Connect to cmlabdc01 or any of the other on-prem lab servers and sign in.

2. Open a web browser and go to the Azure portal (https://portal.azure.com).

3. Sign in with your administrator credential and then use the left navigation menu to go to Azure Active Directory.

4. On the Azure AD page go to *Azure AD Connect*, then select *Download Azure AD Connect*. You will be redirected to a Microsoft download page. Download the installer (.msi file) and then run it.

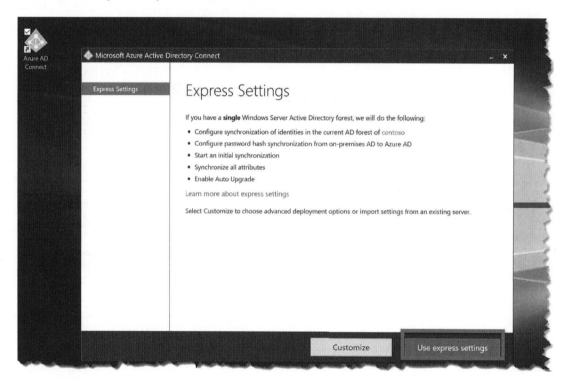

5. Accept the conditions in the setup wizard, review and accept the *Express settings* option.

6. When prompted, enter your tenant administration credentials to connect to the Azure AD tenant and then select *Next*.

7. On the *Connect to AD DS* page, add your Active Directory admin credentials and choose *Next*.

8. On the *Azure AD sign-in configuration* page you will receive a warning that your on-prem domain suffix does not match Azure AD. For our co-management exercise this step is not required so you can select *Continue without matching all UPN suffixes to verified domains*.

Tip! – Set up Active Directory UPN's to match Azure AD

As a bonus step I recommend taking a quick detour at this point to line up Active Directory and Azure AD User Principal Names (UPN's) to make everything seamless for your users. For example, if your Azure AD tenant has a custom domain name of "learningmem.com" and your on-prem AD tenant is called "learningmem.internal" then it could be quite strange for users because they use a different username when logging on to Windows 10 devices on-prem versus when authenticating to cloud services like Office 365.

The good news is that this is easily fixed by adding an alternative UPN to all Active Directory user accounts. To add alternative UPN, launch the *Active Directory Domains and Trusts* tool on a domain controller or another computer with Active Directory Domain tools installed on it. After launching the tool, open it and right-click *Active Directory Domains and Trusts* on the left-nav. Select *Properties* and you will see options to enter one or more UPN suffixes. Type in the suffix that matches your Azure AD tenant name then select *Add* and *Apply*.

After you add an alternative suffix, you can apply this to new or existing AD user accounts in the *Active Directory Users and Computers* tool or in bulk using a script.

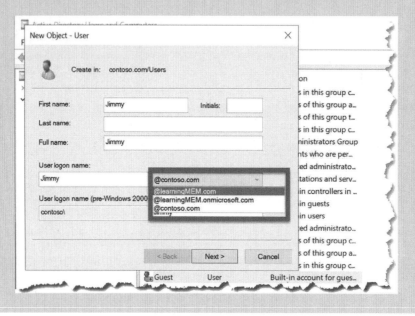

9. Complete the Azure AD Connect setup wizard and then select *Finish* to close the tool.

10. Re-open the Azure AD Connect tool from the desktop and select *Configure > Configure device options > Next* and then provide your tenant administrator credentials.

11. On the *Device Options* page, select *Configure Hybrid Azure AD Join*, then select *Next*.

12. On the *Device Operating Systems* page, select *Windows 10 or later domain-joined systems*.

13. On the *SCP Configuration* page, select the *Consoto.com* domain (or the domain name you are using), then provide credentials for your on-prem Enterprise Administrator.

14. Complete the setup wizard for Hybrid Azure AD Join.

15. After it finishes, return to the Azure AD browser window, on the *Azure AD Connect* page you should see a status of *Connected* now. Any on-prem user accounts (and password hashes) that you create in Active Directory will be synced to Azure AD.

Do it – Turn on co-management for existing on-prem devices

In this exercise you will enable co-management from the Configuration Manager console and move all workloads to be managed by Intune.

1. Connect to *CMlabPS01* and open the Configuration Manager console from the start menu.

2. Go to *Administration > Cloud services > Co-management*.

3. Right-click on the existing *CoMgmtSettingsProd* policy and select *Properties*.

4. Select the *Enablement* tab and change the *Automatic enrollment in Intune* option to *All*.

5. Select the *Workloads* tab and move the sliders for each workload to the *Intune* position. This will ensure that co-managed devices can receive all Intune workloads.

6. Select *Apply* and then *Ok* to close the policy window. Congratulations! You've enabled co-management!

7. It might take some time for the whole co-managed process to complete but eventually Configuration Manager clients will receive the new co-managed policy you just configured. Once they do, they will perform Azure AD Device registration and then MDM enrollment.

8. When devices have become co-managed you will find them in the MEM *All devices* page. Select one and you can view information about which MEM component is configuring workloads.

Tip! – Troubleshooting automatic device registration and automatic enrollment

The process of devices performing a Hybrid Azure AD Join and then enrollment into Intune is not instant – you need to either be patient at this point or hurry things up by initiating Configuration Manager policy sync on devices and rebooting them. You can tell that everything is working because you will see new devices in the MEM admin center labeled as "Co-managed".

If waiting doesn't work for you, there are some tools available for checking the registration and enrollment status:

Windows Event Viewer

Look in the Windows 10 Event Viewer (eventvwr.msc) for Azure AD registration success and failure events: *Microsoft/Windows/User Device Registration*.

Task Scheduler

Look in the Task Scheduler (taskschd.msc), view the history or trigger the tasks manually: *\Microsoft\Windows\Workplace Join\ Automatic-Device-Join*.

Certificate stores

Look in the local certificate store (Certlm.msc) for device registration and MDM certificates:

Registration: Under *Personal/Certificates* look for two certificates issued by *MS-Organization-Access*.

Enrollment: Under *Personal/Certificates* look for a certificate issued by *Microsoft Intune MDM Device CA*.

DSREGCMD

Launch a command prompt (in the context of the actual logged-in user) and launch the built-in utility called *DSREGCMD*. Run the command *dsregcmd /status /debug* to see detailed results.

This Microsoft docs article helps interpret the output from DSREGCMD: http://bit.ly/2KOOWXR.

Co-management log

Look in the co-management handler log on Windows 10 devices to troubleshoot the co-management status and details on workload enablement: *%WinDir%\CCM\logs\ CoManagementHandler.log*

CHAPTER 13

ENDPOINT ANALYTICS

Endpoint Analytics (EA) gives you insight into the experience that end-users are having with the technology you give them to do their jobs. Insights are provided on the most impactful end-user experiences such as startup time. Once you have insights, you can drive improvements through proactive remediation scripts.

Additional capabilities are rapidly being added to Endpoint Analytics, but at the time of writing these are the core areas:

Overall experience score

The overall experience score is an aggregation of things that contribute to a good or bad user experience (including Startup performance and recommended software).

Baselines

Baselines are the way for you to measure improvement over time. You start with a potentially low overall experience score and as you make improvements to devices, you will see this score improve. You can even create new baselines and compare them against an industry median – formed from all the other customers using the feature.

Startup performance

There is nothing more frustrating to end-users than slow boot and login. Users should never have to turn-on their device and then go make a coffee while it powers up. The good news is that this feature captures and aggregates startup performance for your devices. You will end up with overall startup and sign-in scores, as well as individual metrics for each of the core, time-consuming and constrained boot phases including group policy processing and any pesky post-login hanging.

The startup performance reports give you some interesting pivots on the startup data that help you identify bad (slow) devices or models. You can also drill into resource-intensive processes that are active during system boot. These all help you make better decisions for end-user productivity when making purchasing decisions for new devices and enterprise software.

Recommended software

The theory is that your software choices have a big impact on end-user experience. For example, users enjoy using Windows 10 much more than using Windows 7. Microsoft doesn't just decide what software is better for users – this is all based on net-promoter scores in surveys. Besides, if you started a new job tomorrow and the company gave you a clunky device running Windows 7 would you be happy?

Other recommended software that contributes to this score includes Autopilot (users prefer the native OOBE setup experience), Azure AD (users have a better experience with Azure AD features like BitLocker self-service and Windows Hello), cloud management (users have a better experience with cloud management over legacy on-prem management such as group policy for startup performance reasons).

Proactive remediations

Proactive remediations let you deploy scripts to fix common issues proactively. By *proactively*, I mean you can deploy these fixes before users even know they have the issue and call the helpdesk to report it. Your tenant will have some default scripts – these are to address issues many customers face – and you can also build your own. An example of a proactive remediation script provided by Microsoft is one that checks if the device has processed group policy in the last seven days. If it hasn't, it will go ahead and trigger a scheduled task so that users get all the latest, greatest policy and configuration.

The scripts you deploy are all written in a detect-and-remediate way so that you end up with reports that provide information about the number of devices experiencing the issue and the number of devices you were able to fix proactively.

One additional note for the proactive remediation feature is that it requires some premium licensing which is above the most purchased EMS. You'll need one of the Microsoft 365 subscriptions. Don't worry, you'll be prompted for confirmation of this when you go to the Endpoint Analytics page in MEM.

A little history on Endpoint Analytics:

In a former role as a Microsoft Premier Field Engineer (PFE) I would go from customer to customer, helping them with mostly proactive (and a little bit of reactive) support on Microsoft products. One of the most popular engagements, and one I loved the most, was helping IT admins tune boot and logon time for Windows PC's. I would start with a super-detailed analysis of the boot and login process across a small sample of Windows computers, measuring resource usage and bottlenecks in CPU and disk, then look closely at the apps and services that were all fighting for resources. We would look out for any synchronous processes such as group policy and scripts that might be slowing boot down (You would not believe the number of login scripts I found that were written to just pause and wait for something to happen).

The only problem with this boot analysis approach was its scalability. We were manually running some deep analysis tools (xPerf and the Windows Performance Toolkit) on a representative sample of Windows PC's and would come up with some recommendations based on the sample and apply those fixes broadly to all. Eventually, some of my very clever colleagues, led by Matt Reynolds, addressed this by automating the entire boot capture and analysis process. An automated measure and collect system using PowerShell scripts was developed where customers could collect boot traces from a large, distributed sample of PC's automatically and store them centrally for analysis. This system of automated boot tracing was not a Microsoft packaged software product but rather a framework and set of scripts that we Microsoft Field Engineers could use with customers to perform boot analysis and drive some big improvements in their end-user experience.

When Matt changed roles to work in a product engineering team, he took all this knowledge, experience and drive to improve end-user experience and now, many years later, we have Microsoft Endpoint Analytics.

Do it – Try out Endpoint Analytics

In this exercise you will onboard to Endpoint Analytics by deploying an onboarding policy to every enrolled device in the tenant.

1. Go to the MEM admin center and select *Reports* from the navigation menu, then go to *Endpoint Analytics*.

2. On the Endpoint Analytics page, select *All cloud-managed devices* and then choose *Start*. This will cause Intune to create a policy and assign it to all devices (but it will only apply to Azure AD joined or Hybrid Azure AD joined Windows 10 1903+ devices). When they receive the policy, they will start sending analytics data to MEM.

3. Navigate to *Devices > Configuration policies* and find the policy called *Health Monitoring*.

4. Select the policy and then go to *Device status*. A status of *Succeeded* shows that the policy was applied on test devices.

5. Now return to the *Endpoint Analytics* report and start to review the reporting information. It may take up to 24 hours to see *Startup performance* data. You can also view the per-device analytics by navigating to *Devices > All devices > [device name] > Endpoint Analytics*.

Enable ConfigMgr-only devices for EA

If you have devices that are managed only by ConfigMgr (tenant attached) you can enable these for Endpoint Analytics, too. To enable it, just to the *Co-management* settings in the Configuration Manager console. Check the box *Enable Endpoint Analytics for devices uploaded to Microsoft Endpoint Manager*.

CHAPTER 14

TROUBLESHOOTING

You will spend a lot of time troubleshooting in the MEM admin center. This chapter is intended to give you a good overview of various MEM features built to help you figure out what went wrong.

Troubleshooting and support experiences

In the MEM admin center, there is a top-level navigation menu item called *Troubleshooting + support*.

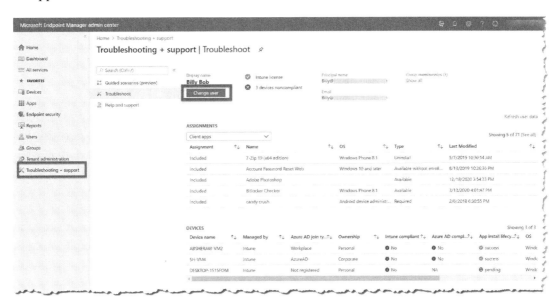

This page hosts an experience built specifically with IT support technicians and helpdesk in mind. The first action a support technician takes is to find the user who is phoning support to report an issue. After selecting an Azure AD user account the technician sees important information about that user:

- Intune licensing information – MEM is not going to work properly if the user is unlicensed.

- Assignments – Apps, compliance policies, configuration policies, app protection, updates, scripts and enrollment restrictions.

- Devices – List of devices that are associated with this user account.

- App protection policy – List of policies and protected apps.

- Enrollment failures – Log entries for failed enrollment for this user account.

The support technician is then able to drill through items on the report to focus on the problem at hand.

Do it – Try out the Troubleshooting + support page

1. Go to the MEM admin center and then to *Troubleshooting + support*.

2. Choose *Select user* and then choose one of the test user accounts you used in previous exercises.

3. Browse through all the available information for this user including the assigned workloads and enrolled devices.

Resource reports

Resource reports are pages that give you detailed information about a *resource*. A *resource*, in this context, could be a single device object or a workload (for example, a single policy, profile or app). The MEM admin center has two main entry points to see these resource reports:

Device resource reports

Device resource reports give you information about what state the device is in – the configuration, compliance policies that applied or failed to apply on a device and in some cases, some detailed information about the error. This detailed information makes these reports a good spot to start if you want to check deployment progress on a given device. If you start troubleshooting in the *Troubleshooting + support* page and select one of the users' devices, you will land on this page to continue the troubleshooting effort.

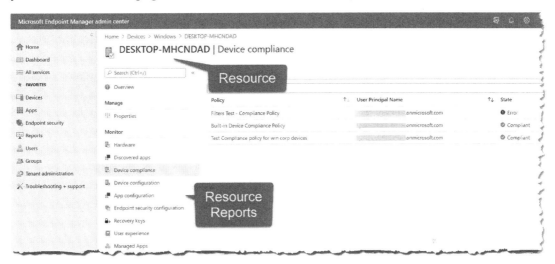

Workload resource reports

Workload resource reports are a good way to troubleshoot a particular workload deployment. For example, if you created a new policy or app and distributed it to a large group, then you come to the resource report for that workload and check that all the in-scope devices were receiving the policy. Almost all MEM workloads have a *Device install status* or *Device status* report that shows each device, its applicability and overall status (success or failure).

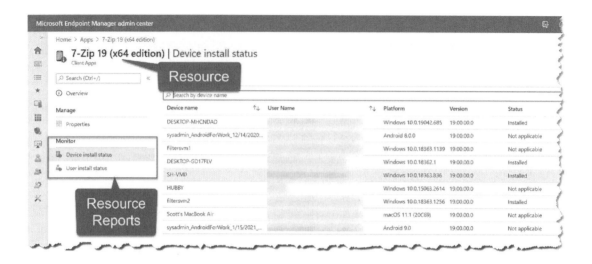

Tip! – Pending status

There are some interesting nuances in workload resource reports worth mentioning:

Device status reports for policy type workloads (configuration, compliance) show device records almost instantly when you target a new group. For each targeted device you will notice *Pending* in the status until the device checks in and updates to either *Succeeded* or *Failed*.

On the other hand, app workloads do not show any device entries in this report until a targeted device has performed an MDM check-in. A status of *Install pending* means that the device received the message and is in the process of installing the app.

Operational reports

Everything under *Apps > Monitor* and *Devices > Monitor* in the menu is known as *Operational level* reports. They are all purpose-built reports that are intended to bubble up workload-specific errors – usually focused on solving a problem. For example, there is a report called *Noncompliant devices* which shows only devices that are currently in a non-compliant state. Similarly, there is an *Enrollment failures* report intended to give visibility to enrollment problems.

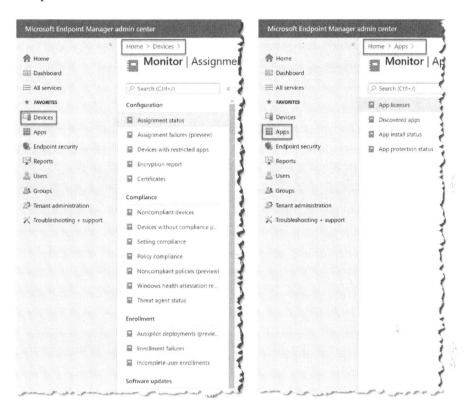

Organization reports

The next group of reports that are useful for troubleshooting are all located in the *Reports* section of the navigation menu and are summarized as *Organizational reports*. These are higher-level reports intended to aggregate the current status of the MEM environment in a way that could easily be used by upper management. They are less focused on troubleshooting specific problems but instead intended to answer key questions such as what percentage of the device fleet is compliant? One of the key functional differences between these reports and the other types is that there is a *Generate* button that can be used to re-build the report based on the latest data instead of being subject to a regular update schedule.

Do it – Try out resource reports

1. Go to the MEM admin center and then to *Devices > All devices*.

2. Select one of the devices from the list.

3. On the *Device* page, browse through the detailed reports for each workload under *Monitor: Hardware, Discovered apps, Device compliance, Device configuration, App configuration, Endpoint security configuration, Recovery keys, User experience* and *Managed apps*.

Client logs

In some cases, you will need to collect client-side information via client logs to fully diagnose issues. Depending on the scenario you are troubleshooting, the following logs might come in handy:

Company Portal app logs

The Company Portal app on each platform (and the Intune app for Android Enterprise device owner scenarios) can capture logs that might help you troubleshoot issues. In some platforms you can view the logs yourself and try to make sense of them but in others you will submit the logs directly to Microsoft support and then when you raise a case, the Microsoft support technician you talk to will be able to retrieve the logs using the code you supply them.

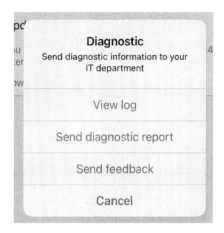

Device logs

Often the root cause of a policy or app installation failure can only be found by looking at device-level logs. While the final error code is available in the MEM admin center it might not give you enough information to decide what to do next. This is where device logs can be helpful:

- **iOS device logs** – You can access device logs only by connecting a device to a macOS device via a lighting cable. Use the *Terminal* app on a macOS device to see detailed information about app installation or the MDM session.

- **Windows device logs** – Use the built-in Windows MDM Advanced Diagnostics Report or Event Viewer to diagnose issues. MEM also keeps a local log file for the Intune Management Extension service responsible for installing Win32 apps and running PowerShell scripts. These are useful locations for you to look at when experiencing errors:

- **Advanced Diagnostic Report** – Shows a detailed client-side view of all the MDM payload delivered during MDM sync sessions. The setting names and values are often displayed in a very raw format so they can be tricky to understand but with some googling you should be able to map these to the settings you configured in MEM. To produce this report, you must go to *Settings > Accounts > Access work or school > Connected to [your company name] Azure AD > Info > Create report*.

- **Device Management Enterprise Diagnostics Provider** – You can see event messages for MDM sessions between the device and MEM and look out for other failures including enrollment errors. My advice is to take *Error* level events with a grain of salt because these appear even on completely healthy devices. You can access this event log by opening Event Viewer and navigating to *Microsoft-Windows-DeviceManagement-Enterprise-Diagnostics-Provider/ Admin*. Microsoft provides a good level of documentation on Windows 10 enrollment errors to watch out for in this log in their online documentation: http:// bit.ly/3tcqFN4.

- **Application event log** – If you find app installation errors returned to the MEM admin center you may need to see the root cause in this log. Open Event Viewer and open *Application* to see the events.

App protection policy – client logs and diagnostics

One of the great features introduced for troubleshooting app protection policy is a diagnostics console that can be viewed from the physical device. The console can be used to view the last policy application time, the protected apps and settings that were delivered. To access the diagnostics console, just install the Microsoft Edge browser on the device and then type *about:intunehelp* in the URL bar. The console will open and give you the option to view the status, including the settings for each app installed on the device and the last policy application details.

6:19

Done   **Intune App Status**

com.microsoft.msapps
com.microsoft.msedge
com.microsoft.Office.Outlook
com.microsoft.Office.Word
com.microsoft.officemobile

MinAppVersionWipe = "0.0";
MinOSVersionWipe = "0.0";
MinOsVersion = "0.0";
MinOsVersionWarning = "0.0";
MinSDKVersion = "0.0";
MinSDKVersionWipe = "0.0";
NonBioPassTimeOutRequired = 0;
NonBioPassTimeout = 60;
NotificationRestriction = 0;
OpenDataFromManagedLocations = 7;
OpenDataIntoOrgDocumentsBlocked = 0;
PINCharacterType = 0;
PINEnabled = 0;
PINExpiryDays = 0;
PINMinLength = 4;
PINNumRetry = 5;
PrintingBlocked = 0;

Audit logs

If you ever suspect that you have a cowboy administrator making changes and causing issues, then a good place to start is MEM Audit Logs. Auditing is on by default and cannot be disabled so you should be able to figure out who is making the unauthorized changes quickly. It shows you all the changes that were made in the MEM admin center or directly to the service in other ways such as scripting. You can export the logs or connect MEM information directly to other log analysis or Security Information and Event Management (SIEM) systems that you already use (for example, Azure Sentinel). To view Audit Logs, go to *Tenant Administration > Audit Logs*.

Getting help from Microsoft

If you still can't figure out what is causing issues you can get help from Microsoft support directly in the MEM admin center. The experience will offer diagnostic options for common issues and links to solutions. If your issue is still not solved, you can log a support case with Microsoft.

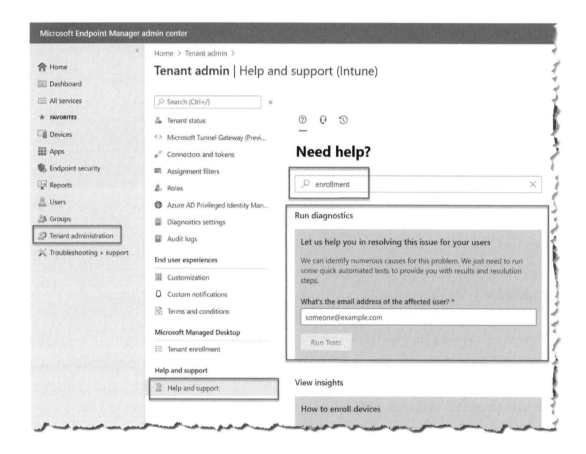

CHAPTER 15

ADVANCED USAGE AND
RESOURCES TO LEARN MORE

In this chapter you will get a taste of MEM's advanced features and extensibility. I will list some bonus learning resources for you to explore further – MEM has an amazing community of IT administrators and Microsoft Valued Professionals (MVPs) who have contributed great content and posted it online to help you, so I will point you to the best places to get the goodies.

Grouping and targeting – Exclude groups

Policy and app assignments to groups are not as simple as they might look. While it *is* simple to assign workloads in the default "Include" mode, there are other options that provide you greater assignment flexibility.

Included and Excluded groups

When you assign a workload in the MEM the default option is an "Included group" assignment. But there is a less-used feature called "Excluded groups". With this feature you can, say, assign a profile to "All Australia Users" as an included group and then "Contractors" as an excluded user group. The result is that the workload is assigned to all Australian users except contractors. It is not supported to mix user groups and device groups – so you cannot, for example, use them to assign to all Australian users except on Samsung devices. See the next section on *Filters* for how to do that.

Role-based access control (RBAC) and Scope tags

RBAC lets you deal with the fact that in most environments you are not the only admin working in the MEM admin center. There are often multiple roles such as Level 1, 2 and 3 support desks, MEM Architects and other teams such as security and identity, and they do not all need the same level of access (privileges) on the same set of devices (Scope). "Least privilege" is a good security principle – Level 1 support desk probably should not have god-mode access to perform actions on all devices and all features because without the proper training and experience they could inadvertently change something tenant-wide and cause significant business impact.

To achieve the least privilege MEM gives you a choice of several "built-in" roles to choose from or you can build your own custom roles:

- **Help Desk Operator** – Primarily used for device management including issuing device remote access commands and assigning resources to groups.

- **Policy and Profile Manager** – Used for creating and editing assignable objects such as configuration policy and apps.

- **Read Only Operator** – As the name suggests this is a set of view only permissions across user, device, enrollment, configuration, and application information.

- **Application Manager** – Can create and manage apps including reports.

- **School Administrator** – This is an education environment-specific role to limit permissions to the minimum needed to operate the Intune for Education portal.

- **Endpoint Security Manager** – Used to control access to everything in the Endpoint Security section of the MEM admin center – compliance, security, baselines and Conditional Access.

Once you decide on a role or build your own, the next step is creating a "Role definition". A role definition is made up of two main parts:

Who – This is the set of MEM administrators that should get the set of privileges defined in the role. This is specified as an Azure AD group of admin user accounts.

What – The MEM groups, devices or resources that these Admins can view and manage in the MEM admin center and perform device actions upon. This administration scope is defined with both groups and scope tags.

The "Who" is pretty straightforward but the "What" gets a little trickier because the scope is defined by two things – groups and scope tags. Groups are just the Azure AD security group of users or devices that an admin can perform actions upon. Scope tags are used to define the individual resources (policies, apps, devices) that an admin can see in the console. An admin can see all the resources matching the scope tags that have been assigned to them via this role assignment.

> **Tip! – Azure AD Roles with permissions in MEM admin center**
>
> It's possible to assign administrators roles in Azure AD which impact their experience while working in the MEM admin center. For example, the Azure AD *Global Administrator* role has permissions to do anything they want across the whole tenant including MEM, Office 365 and any other Microsoft cloud services. The Intune Administrator has full access to everything in the MEM admin center. Review the Azure AD roles that work over the top of the MEM RBAC roles in Microsoft docs: http://bit.ly/2MmUry5

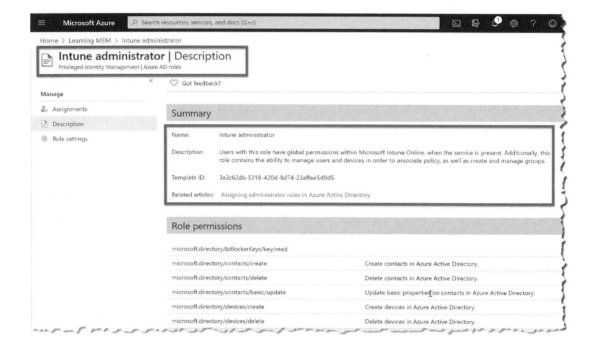

Graph API

Microsoft Graph API is a RESTful API (this means it is a programming interface that uses web requests like GET, POST and DELETE) used across Microsoft cloud services to provide extensibility. Data across Microsoft cloud services is all linked and can be pulled together by crafting the right connections and datasets to achieve interesting scenarios – both for IT professionals and developers. For example, to make your device administration role easier you could create a PowerShell script that pulls data about an Azure AD user (from Azure AD graph) and their managed devices (from MEM). Posting data directly into a graph provides a lot of flexibility and automation – for example you could automate scenarios such as user onboarding or offboarding across all cloud services in the tenant. All tasks that you perform in the MEM console are based on graph API, so if you can do it in the console, you can automate it!

Below are a couple of pointers to get started:

Graph Explorer

You can start to get the hang of graph API using a tool called Microsoft Graph Explorer. On this website, you can use graph queries to get or post data directly into MEM (or other Microsoft cloud services).

Do it – Try out Microsoft Graph Explorer

In this exercise you will use Microsoft Graph Explorer to understand the structure of the data stored in the MEM admin center and see that everything in the MEM admin center (and more) can be viewed and configured via graph.

1. In a new browser tab go to https://graph.microsoft.io.

2. Select *Graph Explorer* from the top navigation menu.

3. Select *Sign in to Graph Explorer* on the left-hand menu.

4. On the *Permissions requested* prompt, accept the permissions required by Graph Explorer.

5. Select *Run query* on the default, pre-populated query (https://graph.microsoft.com/ v1.0/me). Notice that this returns information about the signed-in Azure AD user account from Azure AD.

6. Now try running a query to view all enrolled MEM devices and review the results in Graph explorer:

https://graph.microsoft.com/beta/deviceManagement/manageddevices

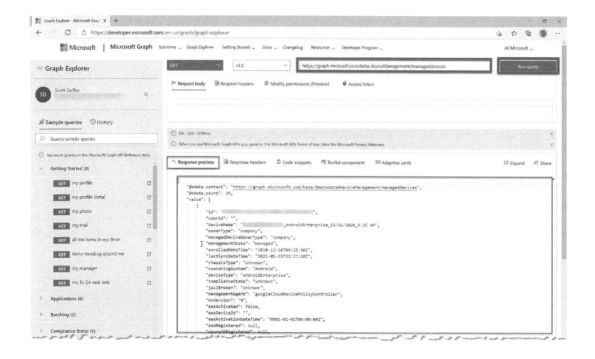

Graph permissions

Did the query fail with a *Forbidden* error message? If so, you need to consent to permissions for Graph Explorer to access the device management graph endpoints. Select the "Cog" (Settings) icon next to your signed-in user account and choose *Select permissions* in the context pane and then consent to each of the permission sets that start with "DeviceManagement".

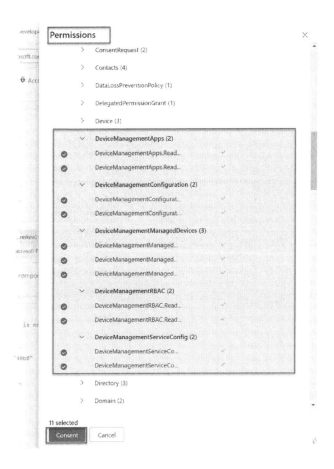

Browser developer tools

The MEM admin center uses Graph API behind the scenes. Everything you see and do in the MEM admin center is built on top of it and browser tools can often give you more insight for troubleshooting. Using browser debugging tools is also a good technique to reverse-engineer graph calls so that you can create your own automation scripts or management apps on top.

Do it – Try out browser developer tools to see Graph API calls

1. Sign in to the MEM admin center and sign in.

2. In your browser, enable browser Developer tools. If you are using the Edge browser, this option is under ... > *More tools* > *Developer tools* or use the F12 keyboard shortcut.

3. Navigate to *Devices* > *All devices* and wait for the page to load the list of devices.

4. In the Developer tools pane, under the *Network* tab, you will notice a lot of different network calls being made by the browser.

5. Look for a network call starting with *ManagedDevices* and select it.

6. View the full Graph API call (Request URL) that was made to return the entire device list. Optionally, you could copy and paste these into Graph Explorer and return the same information.

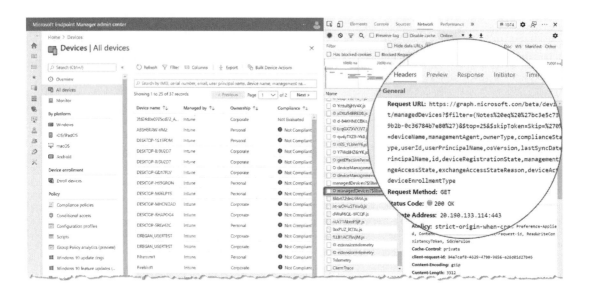

PowerShell scripts and samples

Want to automate with PowerShell? Great news! You don't have to from scratch! You can find PowerShell scripts created by the MEM IT admin and MVP community and directly from the product group. The best place to start is the GitHub repo: http://bit.ly/2YMJeZZ.

Do it – Try out PowerShell for MEM

1. Go to GitHub and search for "Intune PowerShell samples" or follow the short link: http://bit.ly/2YMJeZZ.

2. Select *Code > Download ZIP* to download all scripts.

3. After the download completes, extract the contents into a new folder.

4. Navigate to the *ManagedDevices* folder (…\powershell-intune-samples-master\ ManagedDevices) and open a new PowerShell window as an administrator.

5. In the PowerShell windows launch one of the scripts:

    .\ManagedDevices_Get.ps1

6. When prompted, type the admin username and password for authenticating to your MEM tenant.

7. Accept the permissions in the *Permissions requested* dialog. Like the Graph Explorer tool, PowerShell needs app permissions to make graph changes – this permission request is embedded in the sample PowerShell script in the *Get-AuthToken* function.

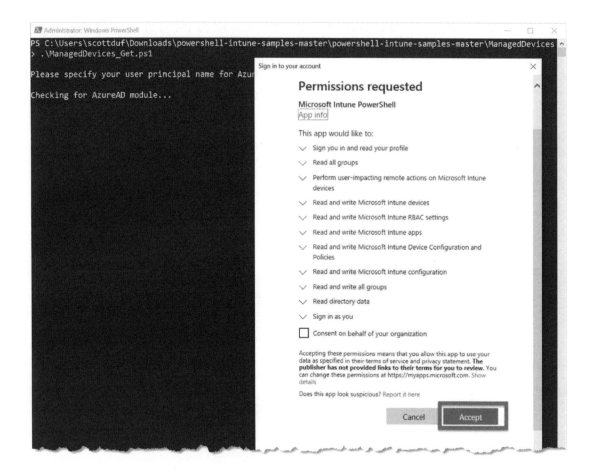

8. You will now see the results – all managed devices listed.

> Try out some of the other sample scripts available – use the documentation in GitHub
> to learn about each script and how to open and customize one.

Advanced reporting and automation

When it comes to reporting, MEM allows you to extend upon what is available in the admin center by exposing the raw data for you to create your own reports or automation. It can be extended through integration with Azure Monitor or the Intune Data Warehouse. MEM events or audit log entries can also be used to trigger other actions. For example, you could automate a process where admins receive an email every time another admin makes a change to a compliance policy, or if device compliance numbers drop below a certain percentage.

Azure Monitor

Azure Monitor is an engine for collecting, storing and analyzing logs. The product has features that let you pull in data from MEM and then do more with it. You can build advanced data visualizations, combine it with other data (for example, data from your SIEM) or pump it out to other data stores – you are only limited by your own creativity. Azure Monitor also has alerting capabilities so that you can automate alerts based on MEM events. Azure Monitor is not included in any of the Microsoft 365 or EMS licensing bundles; the pricing is based on Azure storage account size (to store the events) and Azure Event Hub (number of events being processed).

Data Warehouse

The MEM Data Warehouse feature contains a big pool of data about the devices in your MEM environment. Use it to build your own reports using tools like Microsoft Excel, Microsoft Power BI or any other data visualization tool that supports OData feeds. Microsoft provides a Power BI sample app called Intune Compliance that is a good reference or starting point if you plan to build your own reports.

Do it – Try out Data Warehouse

In this exercise you will use Microsoft's sample Power BI app to visualize your own MEM tenant information. The sample app can be installed from Microsoft's AppSource, which is an app store for Power BI applications.

1. In a web browser, go to http://bit.ly/3pU7PYK or type "Intune Compliance Power BI dashboard" into a search engine.

2. On the *AppSource* page, sign in with your tenant administration credentials if prompted and accept any consent messages.

3. Review the information about the *Intune compliance (data warehouse)* app and then select *Get it now*.

4. On the *Install it now* dialog select *Install*.

5. Wait for the Power BI app to install. When it is complete, select *Go to app*.

6. The default view of the data is based on sample data. Select *Connect your data* in the ribbon, then *Next > Sign in and connect*.

7. Provide your tenant administration credentials if prompted.

8. Refresh the page and you will see familiar device names and information for your own MEM tenant.

9. Click through some of the report pages and explore some of the data available.

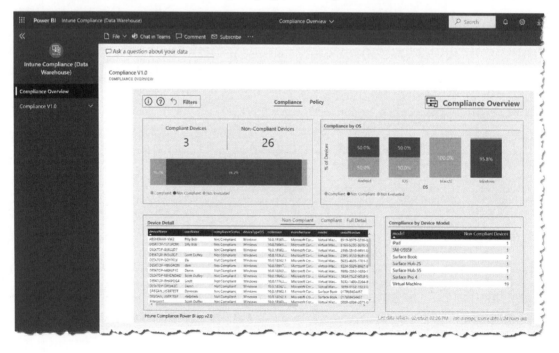

Tips for staying up to date

Staying up to date with MEM can be tricky because the service is updated so frequently with new features. Changes are not limited to the MEM admin center – you have the back-end service and Graph API and then pile on top of that updates to client apps including Microsoft Office mobile apps (that integrated with the Intune App SDK) and the Company Portal or Microsoft Intune mobile apps. The good news is that there are a couple of places you can watch to stay in-the-know on the latest and greatest:

MEM "What's new" and "In-development" docs pages

Microsoft maintains up to date release notes about what rolled out in the last service release (What's new) and what they expect to release next month (In-development). If you do nothing else to stay up to date, I recommend bookmarking this web page and checking it in the last week of every month. Even better, set up an RSS feed so that you receive an email as soon as an update is made to either of these pages.

- MEM What's new – http://bit.ly/3a4fQFf.

- MEM What's new in the apps UI – http://bit.ly/3aOTVAS.

- MEM In-development – http://bit.ly/2MDBHKN.

- MEM Important notices – http://bit.ly/2N8vHJI.

What is your MEM version?

Behind the scenes, MEM is globally rolled out in phases or rings – starting with internal Microsoft environments and then applying to tenants globally. The last phase of MEM service update is a change to the admin center interface which typically occurs the last week of each month. If you want to know which release your tenant is currently running you can view it under *Tenant admin > Tenant details*.

Release numbers are in the format of YYMM, for example 2101 is the January 2021 service update.

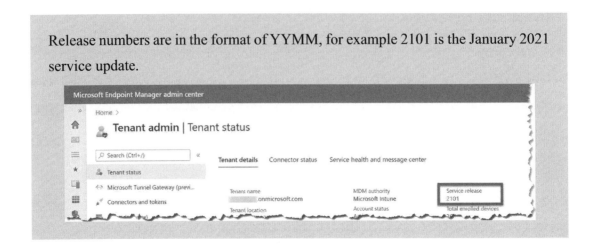

Twitter

Twitter is a great option for staying up to date on new features, but also current issues or outages. There is an amazing community of specialists and Microsoft Valued Professionals (MVP's) who are continuously posting great blogs and tips to help others be successful. Here are my follow recommendations:

- Intune Support Team (@IntuneSuppTeam) – The Intune Support Team Twitter account is owned by Microsoft's own tier 3 support organization. If you follow this account, you will get news about all updates, issues and tips. As a runner-up, the official Twitter account of MEM is @MSIntune but you are much more likely to get marketing content on that one (rather than the nitty-gritty tech details from the support team).

- Intune hashtags (#MSIntune) – Follow the most widely used hashtag for MEM features. You should also check on some related tags such as #MEM, #MEMCM and #AzureAD.

- MSFT MEM Team (https://bit.ly/3snaCui) – Follow this Twitter list to catch tweets from many of the Program Managers and Developers working on the product.

Other social media options

I recommend Twitter over other social platforms because it seems to be the most widely used by Microsoft PM's like myself and many of the IT pros I know. If Twitter is not your jam, there are some other social media options you might consider:

- Reddit – http://bit.ly/2MEZryd.

- Discord – http://bit.ly/3cSPWWL.

- Facebook – http://bit.ly/3rySfCd.

Service Health Dashboard

Stay on top of outage notifications by monitoring the Service Health Dashboard. You can view this either in the Microsoft 365 admin center or in MEM under *Tenant administration > Tenant status*. The dashboard only shows you incidents that impact your tenant.

Additional learning – videos, blogs, books and the MEM community

Now that you have nailed the basics of MEM, I recommend digging deeper into the parts that matter to you and your organization. Some of the best resources for learning are created by our IT pro and MVP community. These are the ones that I have found useful in my travels:

Videos

- **Intune Training on YouTube** (http://bit.ly/3cTDrKp) – A free video training series dedicated to Microsoft Endpoint Manager. Great content created by Steve Hoskings and Adam Gross who are both MEM MVP's.

- **Microsoft Ignite** (http://bit.ly/3a2dmab) – Microsoft Ignite conferences are a goldmine for training material. You can watch videos of Microsoft Program Managers presenting on their feature areas. The easiest way to find these videos is via You-Tube – just browse the Microsoft Ignite channel.

Blogs

- **Microsoft Endpoint Manager Blog** (http://bit.ly/2YVdVMG) – This blog is the official blog for MEM. It has all the marketing announcements about the latest and greatest features.

- **Intune Customer Success blog** (http://bit.ly/3aQR0Ym) – Posts are authored by the MEM support organization and by MEM Program Managers. This is a great blog for deeper technical information. Most new features will also have a supporting blog post that goes deep on how to use and support the feature.

- **MSEndpointMgr blog** (http://bit.ly/3aLkI18) – Posts are written by a bunch of awesome MVP's (Nickolaj Andersen, Maurice Daly, Jan Ketil Skanke, Sandy Zeng, Donna Ryan and Michael Mardahl) and cover everything from Configuration Manager image management to Intune and Autopilot.

- **How to Manage Devices blog (Anoop C Nair)** (http://bit.ly/3ryTJwh) – This blog site features posts from a whole community of experts including Vimal Das, Rajul OS, Karthick Jokirathinam, Regin R, Kannan CS, Gurudatt Vaidya, Debabrata Pati, Sharad Singh, Vishal Goyel, Hareesh Jampani, Nitin Chhabra, Joymalya Basu Roy, Jitesh Kumar, Deepak Rai, Mohan Kumar, Ankit Shukla, Mark Thomas and Anoop C Nair himself. It is definitely worth checking out.

- **OSdeployment.dk blog (Per Larsen)** (http://bit.ly/3tEQ7uK) – Per is a former MEM MVP, turned Microsoft Program Manager.

- **Imab.dk blog (Martin Bengtsson)** (http://bit.ly/2MF33QN) – Martin's imab.dk blog covers a great selection of topics across MEM, Windows 10 and PowerShell.

- **Modern IT – Cloud – Workplace (Oliver Kieselbach)** (http://bit.ly/2MMlRNS)

– Oliver's Modern IT cloud blog has great content on MEM, Windows 10, Azure AD and app management.

- **prajwaldesai.com (Prajwal Desai)** (http://bit.ly/36VQ3Ni) – Prajwal is an MVP who has some great MEM posts on his prajwaldesai.com site.

- **DeployWindows (Mattias Fors)** (http://bit.ly/3tDkamt) – Mattias has some cracking blog posts on his deploywindows.com blog site.

- **Uem4all.com (Courtenay Bernier)** (http://bit.ly/2N6Rwt9) – Courtenay is a Microsoft Program Manager and has written some amazing blog posts and shared code to help you build E2E scenarios on top of the core MEM feature set. It's all there on UEM4all.com.

- **Oofhours.com (Michael Niehaus)** (http://bit.ly/2YY6QuP) – Michael is a former MEM Program Manager and his blog, oofhours.com, is one of the best available technical resources for Windows Autopilot and related features.

Books:

- **MDM: Fundamentals, Security, and the Modern Desktop: Using Intune, Autopilot, and Azure to Manage, Deploy, and Secure Windows 10 (Jeremy Moskowitz)** – Jeremy is famous for Windows management and his latest book on the topic goes deep into modern PC management for Windows 10. In addition to the book, you'll find some gems on his website http://mdmandgpanswers.com and http://policypak.com.

- **Microsoft 365 Security for IT Pros (Michael Van Horenbeeck with Peter Daalmans, Ammar Hasayen, Ahmen Nabil, and Damian Scoles)** – If you are interested in the security side of endpoint management then check out the book at https://m365securitybook.com).

Final thoughts

Congratulations and thank you for making it to the end of this book! I really enjoyed putting this information together for you and hope it puts you on the right path to becoming a world-class MEM ninja. If this book helped you, please let me know – Leave a review or send me an email at contact@learningMEM.com.